THE ROYAL CANAL

The Complete Story

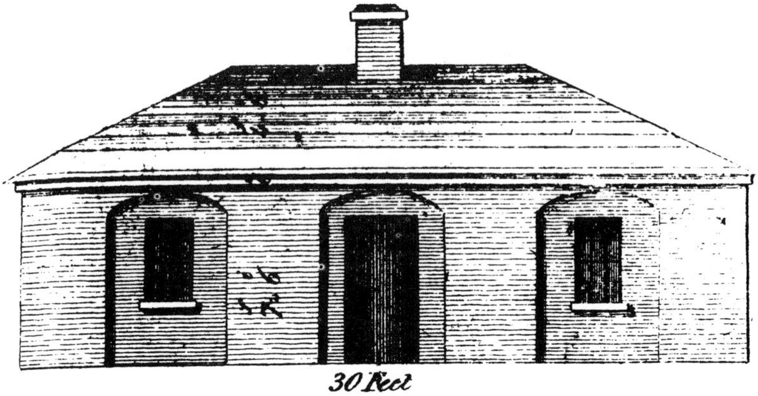

Front Elevation of Lockhouse for Royal Canal western section (I.E.I).

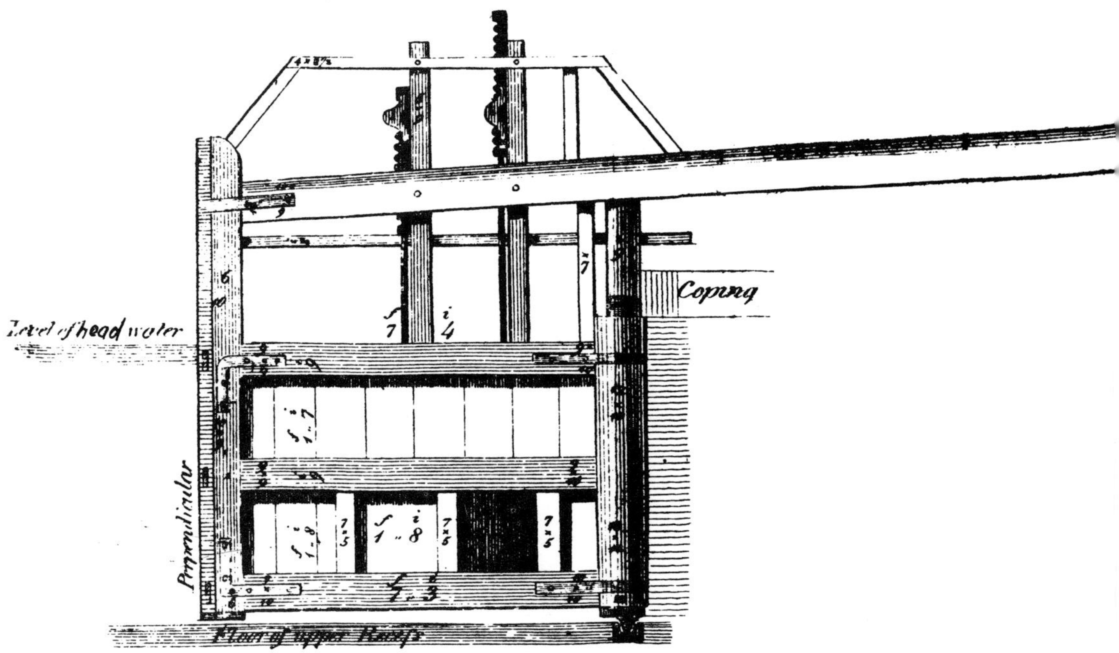

Elevation of Upper Lock Gate for Royal Canal western section (I.E.I.).

The Royal Canal

The Complete Story

Peter Clarke

ELO PUBLICATIONS
October 1992

First published in Ireland, October 1992, by
Elo Publications
Reuben Avenue, Dublin 8

ISBN 0 9519593 2 8

The Maps used in this book are based on the Ordnance Survey by permission of the Government (permit no. 5653).

Media Conversion and typesetting in Garamond Original by Diskon Technical Services Ltd.
Book Designed by Patrick Funge and printed at the Elo Press Ltd., Dublin 8.
Cover photographs by Níall Funge

Dedication

This book is dedicated to the members of the
Royal Canal Amenity Group
whose commitment to and love of
the Royal Canal
has saved it and ensured
its survival for future generations.

Acknowledgements

I would like to thank the following for permission to use their photographs and illustrations. Mr. Tom Darcy, Mr. Eddie Slane, Dr. Ian Bath and Mr. Arnie Poole of the Royal Canal Amenity Group. Ms. Mary Clarke and the City of Dublin Archive. Thomas Pakenham, Tullynally Castle, county Westmeath. The Librarian and Committee of the Irish Railway Record Society. The Council of the National Library of Ireland. Mr. John Haughton who photographed the swans at Reilly's Bridge and Mr. Finbar Callanan and the Institution of Engineers of Ireland. Mr. Níall Funge for his interest and photographs.

Over the six years of researching the historical geography of the Royal Canal many people gave me valuable assistance and help. I would like to take this opportunity to express my appreciation to the following:

The Secretary and Staff of Coras Iompair Éireann, Heuston Station. The Library Staff, Trinity College, Dublin and the staff of the Waterways Division, Office of Public Works. Mr. Matthew Stout who computerised the maps and my good friend Chris Walker whose expertise and help with the computer were invaluable and much appreciated. Sr. Bríd Greville, Paddy Coyle and Eddie Slane for their assistance with proof-reading. Mr. Pat Funge and his staff at Elo Press/Elo Publications for their support in making the book possible.

I am also most grateful to Dr. James Killen and Professor J. H. Andrews, Trinity College, Dublin for their encouragement and advice during the long period of research.

Finally I would like to thank my wife Catherine and my children Peter, Damien and Eleanor for their support and understanding during the preparation of the work.

Contents

List of Illustrations

Frontispiece

(Top) Front Elevation of Lockhouse for Royal Canal western section.
(bottom) Elevation of Upper Lock Gate for Royal Canal Western section.

Black and White Illustrations

Foreword

The story of the Royal Canal is full of surprises. Construction began in 1790 but for a number of reasons, the main line did not reach its final objective, the river Shannon, until 1817. Just twenty-eight years later, the canal was purchased by the Midland Great Western Railway Company which intended to close it and to construct a railway on its bed. In the event, this did not happen; instead, the canal continued to carry traffic with the last freight boat operating as late as 1951. At this time, the future of the waterway seemed bleak; yet today, just forty years later, the eastern section of the canal is restored to traffic and plans exist to re-open the whole route.

In this book, Peter Clarke sets out for the first time the detailed story of the Royal Canal from its beginnings to the present day. His account is based on his intimate knowledge of the canal and upon detailed research undertaken over a number of years. It is informative and eminently readable. Like many good novels, it contains elements of intrigue, frustration, the unexpected and, most satisfying of all, a happy ending! This book will be enjoyed by all of those with an interest in this part of our national heritage.

James E. Killen,
Department of Geography,
Trinity College, Dublin.

Chapter One

Introduction

From 1498 attempts were made in Ireland to develop river and canal navigation but very little progress was made until the early eighteenth century when a formal structured approach developed with regard to inland navigation. In 1715, an Act[1] was passed in the Irish House of Commons "To encourage the draining and improving of the bogs and unprofitable low grounds, and for easing and dispatching the inland carriage and conveyance of goods from one part to another within this kingdom." It was proposed in this Act that large numbers of rivers in all four provinces be made navigable and be linked via a series of navigable channels. While the main aim of the Act was to develop the bogs and waste ground of the Midlands, it was envisaged that the opening of navigable canals and rivers would improve communications throughout the country and increase the prospects of economic development.

No parliamentary funds were allocated for the proposed works. A number of commissioners or undertakers made up of members of parliament and justices of the peace in whose counties the developments were to take place were appointed to raise finances privately and to oversee the work. They were empowered to charge tolls on the completed navigations, these not to exceed two pence for every hundredweight of goods carried and three pence for every passenger carried for a distance of ten miles. Manure for use as fertiliser was to be exempt from tolls while such building materials as timber, stone and bricks were to be charged at half-price.

Little came of these ambitious projects. Work commenced on the river Maigue near Adare, county Limerick[2] and also on the river Liffey between Lucan, county Dublin and Leixlip, county Kildare.[3]

As the financing of these projects was to be raised by the commissioners and because of the high cost of many of the projects, little was achieved by the Act, although it can be said to mark the beginning of canal development in Ireland.

The failure of the 1715 Act to encourage private bodies to construct navigations influenced the Irish Parliament in 1729, by the Act 3 Geo. II c.3,[4] to establish four bodies of unpaid commissioners, one for each province, to replace those appointed under the 1715 Act. In the preamble to the 1729 Act, it was recognised that the 1715 Act had failed. It was felt that this new Act would be more beneficial because it was to be funded by parliament. Funding was actually to be carried out under what were called "Tillage Duties" which were to be raised on a number of luxury goods such as coaches, berlins, calashes and chairs and wrought and manufactured gold and silver plate which were being imported into or were being made in Ireland at the time. It was hoped that the developments caused by the Act would encourage tillage and give employment to the poor.

The 1729 Act did achieve some results. The Newry Canal, linking Newry to Lough Neagh, was constructed between 1731 and 1742[5] while work on the Coalisland Canal was commenced in 1733 but was not completed until 1755 due to engineering difficulties.

In 1751 by the Act 25 Geo. II c.10, the commissioners appointed in 1729 were incorporated into a single navigation board and called The Corporation for Promoting and Carrying on Inland Navigation. The power to appropriate "Tillage Duties" was extended for twenty-one years. The position of the commissioners was legally strengthened under this new Act, particularly with regard to their powers to acquire land to be used for navigation works. The Act laid down clearly how the Corporation should function. It was specified that the main body should meet four times a year and that twenty-four assistant commissioners, six per province, should be elected annually. Provision was made for setting up a full-time central establishment with paid officers, a secretary, a treasurer and clerks. The most important developments which took place under the 1751 Act were the starting of work on the Shannon Navigation in 1755, the construction of the Grand Canal in 1756 and the development of the Barrow and Boyne Navigations in 1759.[6]

On 8 October 1755, a Parliamentary Committee was appointed[7] to consider further laws necessary "for the improvements of Commerce and Inland Navigation" by means of increased tillage and by providing for the planting of trees and the enclosing and preserving of woods. On 1 November the committee reported[8] that the export of corn and grain, with a bounty when prices were low, would promote tillage in the country. On 8 November the committee further reported[9] that "The making of an Inland Navigation from the city of Dublin to the river Shannon by affording an early carriage for corn and timber from the innermost parts to the Capital of this Kingdom will be the most effectual means to increase tillage, and to encourage and promote the planting of trees". It was urged that such a navigation be carried out immediately if found to be practical.

In 1755, £20,000 was allocated to the Navigation Board towards the cost of carrying out the work along the chosen route[10] and two schemes were considered.[11] One was to begin at the City Basin and to proceed on the south side of the river Liffey to join the river Barrow and the river Brosna from where it would enter the Shannon. The second scheme was also a mixture of canal and river navigations. It was to begin at the north-west end of Dublin and to pass through Castleknock to the Rye Water at Kilcock and from there to join the rivers Blackwater, Boyne, Deal, Yellow and, through Lough Derravaragh, the rivers Inny and Camlin from whence it would enter the Shannon (Fig. 1).

Surveys were carried out on both these schemes during 1755 and early 1756. The southern route was surveyed by Thomas Omer[12] on an undisclosed date and he was

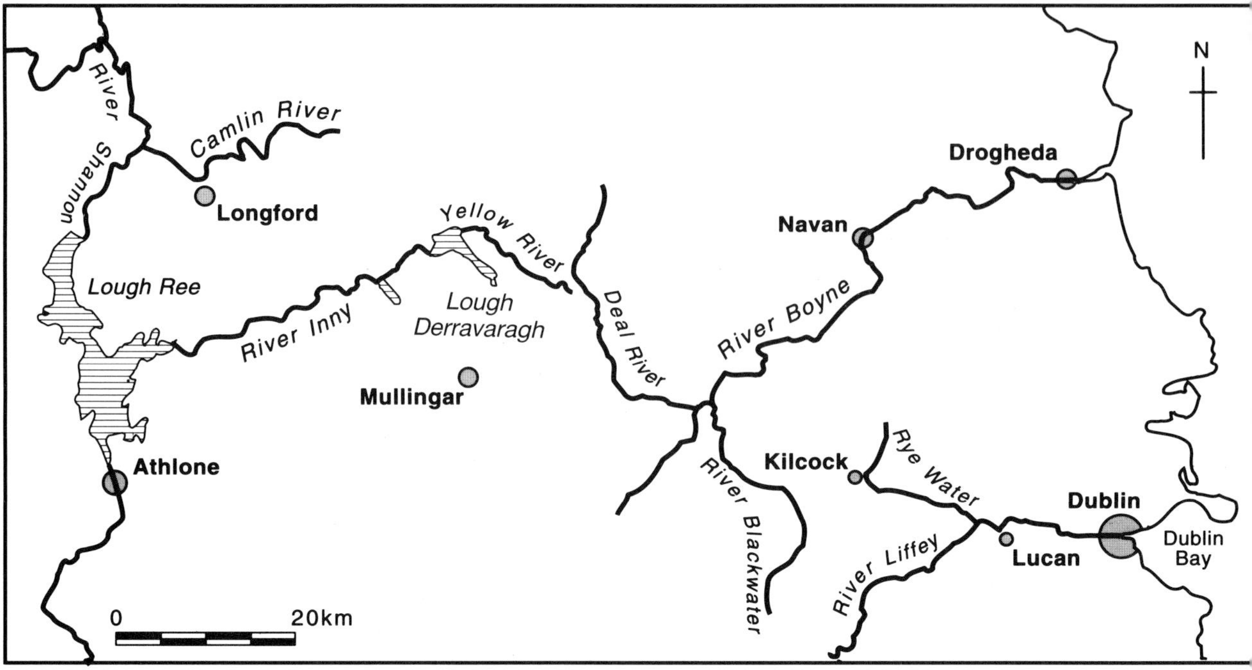

Figure 1: Proposed rivers to be made navigable, 1755.

paid a fee of £200 plus £78-1-8 expenses for his work. The northern route was surveyed by Thomas Williams and John Cooley between 14 August 1755 and 16 January 1756.[13] The complete network of rivers and proposed canals mentioned previously was surveyed and surveys were prepared also on two possible routes to Dublin from Moyglare, county Kildare. Beginning at Moyglare, it was proposed to make the Rye Water navigable to Leixlip and then to cut a canal from there to Dublin. The second proposed route involved constructing a canal from Moyglare through Dunboyne, county Meath, and on to Ballybough in Dublin. Williams and Cooley were paid £78-1-8 plus £31-9-8 expenses for their work.

Considerable debate arose between the promoters of the two different lines of navigation as to which one was most advantageous and a number of pamphlets were published promoting each.[14] By a very small majority in parliament, the £20,000 was awarded to the southern line[15] and thus the Grand Canal project was initiated.

In May 1785, a Committee of the Irish House of Commons[16] reported on the state of Inland Navigation in Ireland. It was their opinion that the money appropriated to inland navigation was "distracted among many objects" and that it was therefore insufficient to complete any works. It was suggested that all funding should be diverted to one navigation and the Grand Canal which was already complete as far as the river Barrow at Monasterevin, county Kildare, was nominated. It was suggested also that consideration should be given to making the river Shannon navigable from Lough Allen to below Limerick city. It was also recommended that the Navigation Board set up in 1751 be disbanded.

Investigation into the affairs of the Navigation Board had been ongoing for many years[17] and had revealed many irregularities. By 1785, the recommended funding was overdrawn by £26,284-17-8 and, in addition, warrants had been issued for payments of a further £22,073-8-9. By Act 27 Geo III c.30 the Navigation Board was dissolved and replaced by separate bodies of commissioners which were appointed for the Newry and Tyrone canals, and the rivers Boyne, Barrow and Shannon respectively. The Grand Canal Company had been formed into a corporate body in 1771-2 and thus the waterways under its control were no longer the responsibility of the Navigation Board.

The transferring of the incomplete navigations to local bodies did little to advance the cause of inland navigation in the country. Because they had no government funding the new bodies were forced to rely on the small income from tolls in order to survive and to complete the works.

The failure of the new bodies to surmount their financial difficulties led parliament to introduce a debenture scheme in 1788 to help finance private companies to build canals.[18] Loans at four per cent were offered on one-third of the total cost of a project, paid in instalments when proof was furnished that double the instalment had been spent. Rules and regulations to be observed by those making application to the House for consideration were also drawn up.

Under this new scheme a series of navigations emerged in Ireland. Among them was a re-vamped version of the northern route river/canal navigation first proposed in 1756. This project was to become the Royal Canal.

Chapter Two

The Beginning of the Royal Canal 1789-1790

The Royal Canal links the city of Dublin to the river Shannon at Cloondara in county Longford. The main line of the canal passes through Dublin city and county, and counties Kildare, Meath, Westmeath and Longford passing through Castleknock, Leixlip, Maynooth, Kilcock, Enfield, Mullingar, Coolnahay, Ballynacarrigy, Abbeyshrule, Keenagh, and Ballymahon. The main water supply to the canal is Lough Owel, entering the canal on the north side of Mullingar, county Westmeath. The summit level of the canal starts at the 25th lock near Riverstown Bridge, county Westmeath, and continues for fifteen miles to Coolnahay six miles beyond Mullingar. The main line is ninety miles long with a branch five miles long linking it to Longford town.[1](Fig. 2). A second branch three-quarters of a mile long linked the main line to the canal harbour at Broadstone. This is now filled in and converted to a linear park.

The Royal Canal like the Grand Canal was one of the most capital intensive projects to be undertaken in Ireland at the end of the eighteenth and beginning of the nineteenth centuries.[2] Construction began in 1790 and was not completed until 1817 at a final cost of almost £1.5 million (equivalent to approximately £85 million at present-day values).

As would be expected on a project of this size, problems arose throughout its construction. Between 1790 and 1811 an extraordinary number of difficulties were encountered. By 1794 with only fifteen miles of canal built, the entire capital of the company had been absorbed and it was bankrupt.

Many of the problems could have been and should have been avoided. The line of canal initially chosen by the

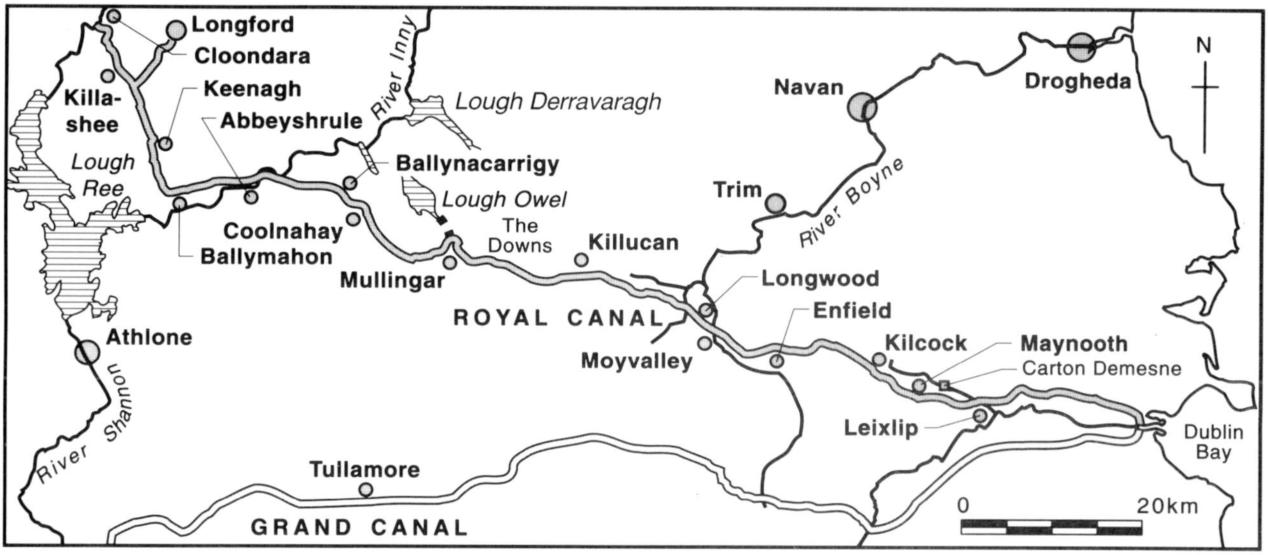

Figure 2: Map of the Royal Canal showing the existing route from Dublin to the Shannon river.

company, although clearly defined on a map presented to parliament with a petition for financial assistance in 1789, was not determined by a survey. Rather, it was pieced together using information from parts of the previous survey undertaken in 1755. The financial estimate for building the canal was also defective as it was not based on accurate information.

The Formation of the Royal Canal Company

The Royal Canal Company was formed in 1789 in response to parliament's decision in 1788 to make funds available in the form of financial aid to persons intending to build canals, make rivers navigable and improve ports and harbours.[3] Who the prime motivator was in forming the company has led to much speculation over the years. In his book *Lives of the Engineers*,[4] Samuel Smiles states "that the canal owes its beginnings to a retired shoemaker and director of the Grand Canal Company who, after a disagreement with his fellow directors, set about starting a canal of his own". Securing the support of the gentry through whose land the intended canal would pass, he eventually succeeded in obtaining an Act of Parliament authorising the construction of the Royal Canal. Smiles's story cannot be substantiated. A comparison of the names of the Royal Canal subscribers and the listed merchants and traders in *Wilson's Dublin Directory*[5] of 1789 yields

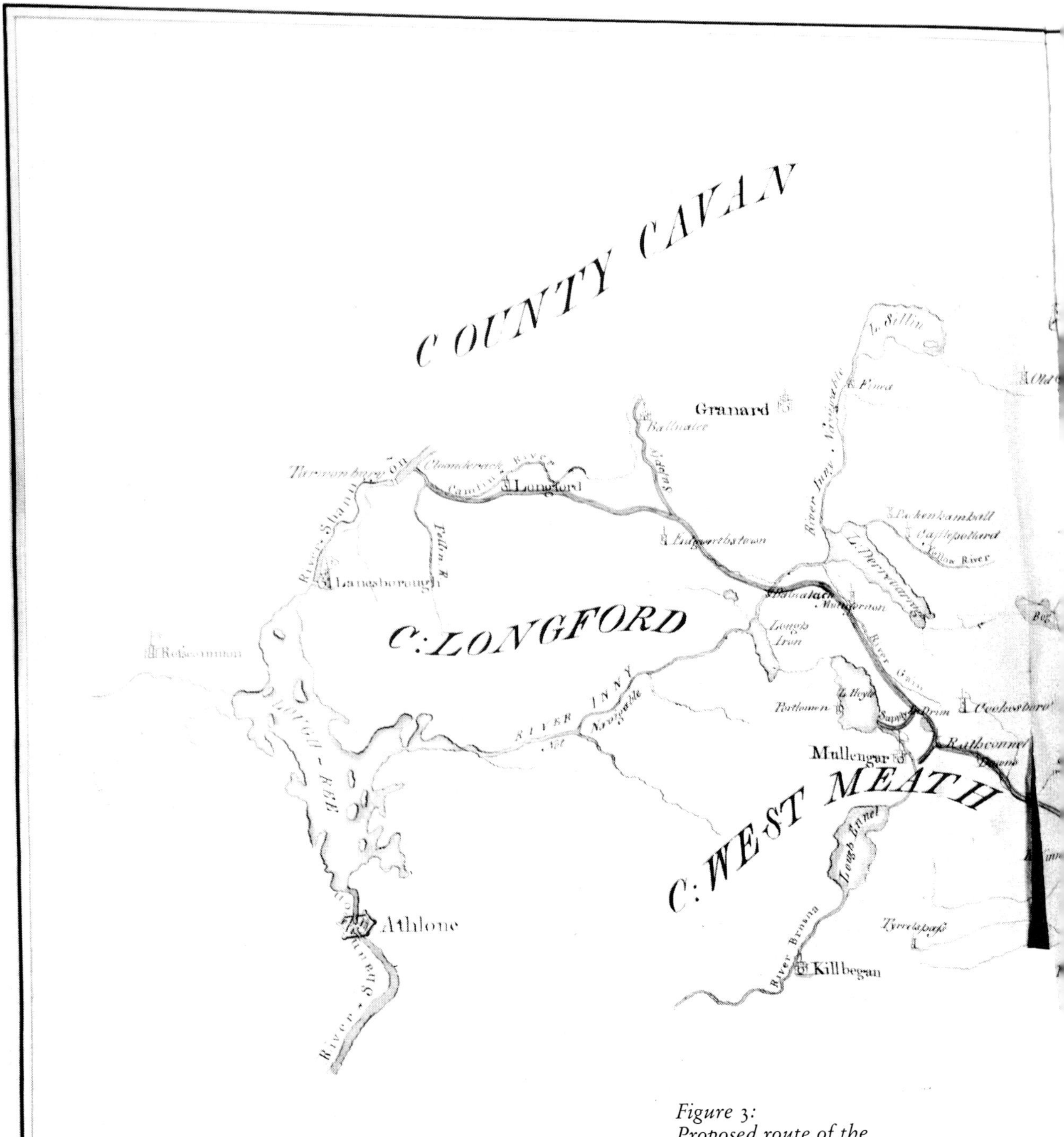

Figure 3:
Proposed route of the Royal Canal, c.1789-90.
(National Library of Ireland)

C: LOUTH
Drogheda
Drogheda Bay
Mellifont
Kells
Black Water
Slane
River Boyne
Nanny Water
Duleek
IRISH
Navan
Athboy
COUNTY MEATH
Trim
Ratoath
Dangan
Summerhill
SEA
C: DUBLIN
Howth
Kilcock
Carton
Leixlip
DUBLIN
Dublin Bay
Carbery
Donadea
C: KILDARE

only two names associated with the shoemaking trade: Edward Clarke of Capel Street Dublin and Ralph Mulhern of High Street Dublin, both listed as shoemakers and both listed as representing the shoemaking trade on the Common Council.[6] Neither is listed as a director of the Grand Canal Company.[7]

No company records of the Royal Canal Company between the years 1789 and 1813 have survived. The primary sources of information available for this period consist of the Irish House of Commons Journals, newspapers and a small number of pamphlets. It is therefore impossible to be precise as to who instigated the subscription. However the name most frequently cited in connection with the company's affairs during this period is John Binns.

Binns, a director of the Grand Canal Company, was also in partnership with William Cope in the silk trade in Shaw Street, Dublin.[8] Cope is also listed as a canal subscriber. As will be seen later, Binns's influence on the early development of the canal was substantial. William Crosbie, a listed canal subscriber, testified to a committee in 1811 that Binns was the principal promoter of the canal and had induced him to subscribe.[9]

The majority of the bridges between Dublin and Mullingar were named after the company directors. However, it is worth noting that the fourth bridge built over the canal is named after John Binns, as it was the closest bridge to his home in Dorset Street.

The Proposed Route

The subscribers to the Royal Canal Company petitioned parliament on the 13 March 1789[10] proposing to build a canal which was to begin at the river Liffey near the new Custom House and continue to Moyglare near the village of Kilcock. At Moyglare [11] the navigation was to divide into two parts, one to run near to Trim and on to Kells, with a branch from Trim to Athboy and Castletowndelvin (Delvin), while the other was to continue on towards Cloncurry, Blackwater bridge and Rathconnell and thence to Tarmonbarry in county Longford and the river Shannon. The route shown on Fig. 3 corresponds to this route. Although the map has no title, date or signature it is likely that this map is a copy of the one presented to parliament with the company's original petition. It is worth noting that the canal shown on the map runs to the north of Carton Demesne and that Mullingar town is served by a branch, somewhat different from today where the canal runs on the south side of Carton and through Mullingar. The proposed canal was to be one hundred and nine miles long with seventy-six locks, eighty-five aqueducts and eighty-five bridges. The estimated cost was £197,098.

Those applying for parliamentary funds were bound by rules and regulations laid down by the orders of the House of Commons of March 1788.[12] These required that each petition be accompanied by a plan describing the proposed route, details of which were to be published in three newspapers one month before the petition was presented. An estimated cost of the proposed work was also required. Also to be included was a separate estimate for the locks, bridges and aqueducts and a list of subscribers and the amount subscribed by each. The petition was to be signed by those making it.

There were one hundred and eighty-eight subscribers for the Royal Canal, the largest subscription promised being £2,000 and the smallest £100.[13] The principal undertakers of the canal were the Duke of Leinster, the Earl of Carhampton, Viscount Ranelagh, Baron Longford, Baron Sunderlin, Sir John Blacquiere, Sir William Gleadowe Newcomen, Thomas Fetherston, John Hatch, Francis Fetherston, William Alexander, James Ormsby, Jasper Debrisay, William Wright, William Cope, John Binns, Thomas Andrews and James Connolly.

A parliamentary committee[14] appointed to examine the petition interviewed John Binns and the eminent land surveyor John Brownrigg of Grafton Street, Dublin. All the members of this committee are not known but it included Captain Thomas Pakenham, brother of Baron Longford, and Mr. Henry Steward. The function of the committee was to ensure that all the relevant documents were received on time and, most important, to establish the viability of the project.

Although Sir John Blacquiere is not cited as a committee member, it must be assumed that he was one as he reported on the committee's behalf back to parliament[15] that the company had complied with the orders of the House of March 1788. By Statute 29 George III c.33 the company was granted the sum of £66,000 which was approximately one-third of the estimated cost of building the canal.

There are indications that very little planning or thought went into preparing the documentation for the initial petition for it was quickly followed by two more seeking additional financial help. The second petition was presented to parliament on 18 April 1789.[16] On this occasion, the company was seeking aid to build graving docks at the termination of the canal on the river Liffey in accordance with plans prepared by the engineer William Jessop. This petition stressed that these docks would be of great advantage to the trade and commerce of Dublin city. The amount of money requested was £32,497 which was half the estimated cost of building the docks. The company offer no explanation as to why the cost of constructing the graving docks was not included in the first petition. In reality, the idea of building graving docks did not emerge until a similar plan[17] was launched by the rival Grand Canal Company. That company had sought aid on 16 April 1789 to build floating docks on the south side of the river Liffey. By the 20 April they had amended their petition with a new one increasing the amount of money sought.[18]

In a similar manner, the Royal Canal subscribers amended their Petition[19] on the same day. In this, their third Petition, an explanation is offered as to why it was being presented. Sir William Newcomen who, on behalf of the subscribers presented the petition to parliament, explained that they had learned with satisfaction that the House had entertained a petition from subscribers for floating docks on the south side of the river Liffey. The Royal Canal subscribers were seeking leave to correct their estimate presented for a similar purpose. In their opinion, they were justified in doing so as it was well known that works of every kind generally exceed their estimate and that in works of this nature it is more likely to happen. They therefore hoped that the House would extend the same indulgence towards them and grant them an additional sum of £10,833. Both petitions were successful although only £24,633 was granted of the £32,497 requested while the full £10,833 was allowed.

The Failure of the Estimate

By 1794 the Royal Canal Company was bankrupt. Both the subscribers' money and parliamentary aid which amounted by then to a total of £197,098 had been spent.[20] A further sum of £7,000 which had been advanced towards building the docks had also been used. Several factors contributed to this situation of which faulty construction and engineering were partly to blame. However, the principal cause of the company becoming bankrupt was that the cost of building the canal had been underestimated in 1789. As stated already, the estimate provided by the company at that time was not based on a detailed analysis of the proposed route but rather was concocted from a variety of sources by John Binns. How the estimate was formed did not emerge until 1796.

The company at that stage was in severe financial difficulties and was forced to seek further aid from parliament.[21] A committee appointed by parliament to examine their petition interviewed John Binns. It was only at this stage that the details of how the estimate and other documentation were pieced together in 1789 emerged. The first plan of the proposed route had been drawn up by John Brownrigg in 1789. He did not take any levels or draw sections. No general survey of the entire route was carried out before the company petitioned parliament. Only one small survey was undertaken on a section of the proposed line when serious doubts arose as to its suitability.

The estimate provided by the company in 1789 was calculated by John Binns with help from James McMahon, a contractor and Thomas Black, a stone-cutter, both employed by the Grand Canal Company. The specification outlined by Binns to Black and McMahon was for a small canal. It was to be four to six feet deep and eighteen feet wide at the bottom. It is unlikely that these dimensions reflected what Binns intended to build: the canal when completed was twenty-four feet wide at the bottom, forty-two feet wide at the top with six feet of water.

On the specification provided by Binns, McMahon estimated that he could cut the canal in favourable ground for £500 per mile and for £800 per mile in less favourable ground. Similarly, Black estimated that he could build the locks for £900 each. The estimated costs of building the bridges and aqueducts are not known. As previously stated, the canal was to be one hundred and nine miles long with seventy-six locks. Assuming that Binns calculated the costs for digging between favourable and unfavourable ground at £650 per mile it would have cost £139,250 to cut the canal and build the locks, leaving only £57,848 to purchase the land and build the eighty-five bridges and aqueducts.

No comparison appears to have been made between the proposed work and the costs incurred on the partly completed Grand Canal. In the thirty-one mile stretch between Dublin and Monasterevin in county Kildare completed in October 1785,[22] there were twenty-six locks, two large aqueducts and twenty-four bridges, which cost £340,000 to complete.[23] As Binns had been a director of the Grand Canal Company from 1772 to 1790, he would have been aware that the cost of the Dublin to Monasterevin section was estimated originally at £60,000. Although extensive surveys were carried out before this estimate was prepared, it still cost more than five times the estimate. Without a comprehensive survey, he must have realised that it would be impossible to know with certainty whether the Royal Canal could follow the proposed route and that it would be impossible to estimate the cost of building the canal accurately without a detailed survey. Most certainly, the estimated cost per mile of the complete project, £198,000 for 109 miles or £1,868 per mile seems remarkably optimistic when compared with the actual cost of £340,000 for 31 miles (£10,968 per mile) of constructing the first thirty-one miles of the Grand Canal.

A typical survey to be carried out prior to the construction of a canal is described by Charles Vallencey in a book published in 1763.[24] "The ground should be frequently bored where the canal is to be dug in order to avoid if possible all bogs and rocks which exceedingly increase the expense of building the canal." Vallancey also recommended that cross-sections be cut across the line at intervals along the proposed route to establish the type of soils that would be encountered during construction. The survey should also include the levelling of the ground to establish the depths to which the canal should be excavated and recommendations concerning the positioning of locks, bridges and aqueducts. In the absence of such a survey, the Royal Canal Company could not have been in a position to anticipate problems which would arise during construction when parliament was being petitioned on the cost of the work.

The line chosen by the company for the canal was similar to the northerly canal/river route surveyed in 1755. In 1789, at the time parliament was being petitioned for the first time, Binns sought the advice of John Brownrigg on the possibility of building a canal from Dublin to the Shannon via county Westmeath. He planned to use part of the earlier 1755 survey which he had acquired. Brownrigg was one of the most noted surveyors in the country and had extensive experience in canal surveying. On a survey for the Grand Canal Company from Robertstown, county Kildare, to Tarmonbarry, county Longford in 1785-6, he had noted that Lough Owel near the town of Mullingar had sufficient water to supply a canal. It was he who suggested that the lake should be used as the primary water supply for the Royal Canal and that it should serve Mullingar.[25] Brownrigg strongly denies being involved in the preparation of the documents used in the estimate but he did carry out a survey of the proposed line at a later stage.

The only survey carried out prior to the Royal Canal Company submitting their estimate to parliament in 1789 was in connection with the water supply. Brownrigg was doubtful if an ample supply could be got before the canal reached Mullingar and Lough Owel. He undertook a survey in the Bog of Cappagh close to Kilcock and

Figure 4: The Royal Canal passing through the Bog of Cappagh showing one of the few remaining mile-stones which mark the distance from Dublin.

ascertained that by sinking about forty feet it would be possible to divert part of the river Blackwater into the canal for use as a feeder. He also calculated the number of locks, bridges and aqueducts which would be required for the canal. However as no detailed survey of the complete course of the proposed canal was carried out prior to the parliamentary petitions, we must accept that the numbers involved were a guess.

The First Detailed Survey

It was not until after the company was granted aid by parliament that Brownrigg was commissioned to carry out the first formal survey.[26] The instructions given to him by Binns were to find the most direct way from Dublin to county Longford and the river Shannon. When exactly the survey commenced is not known: the most likely date is April or May 1789 by which time the weather would have improved. The survey was completed in late November 1789.

The first major problem encountered by Brownrigg was Carpenterstown quarry near the village of Castleknock, county Dublin. This large mass of limestone rock was described by Brownrigg as a "stumbling block of the most serious nature." In his attempt to avoid it, he levelled to its north side through Mulhuddart, county Dublin, and also to the south of it. Both routes presented problems and he decided that the canal would have to run through the quarry.

His instructions were to bring the line as close to the villages of Lucan and Leixlip as the ground would permit. In his attempt to comply with these instructions, he met with further difficulties, finding that the ground beyond Clonsilla towards Lucan and Leixlip was considerably lower than the lands at Castleknock and Carpenterstown. To avoid a high embankment at Lucan, he kept to the north of the village on high ground, proceeding north of Confey Castle and from there to the south of Mulrooney Hill, passing the Rye Water on the left. Keeping north of

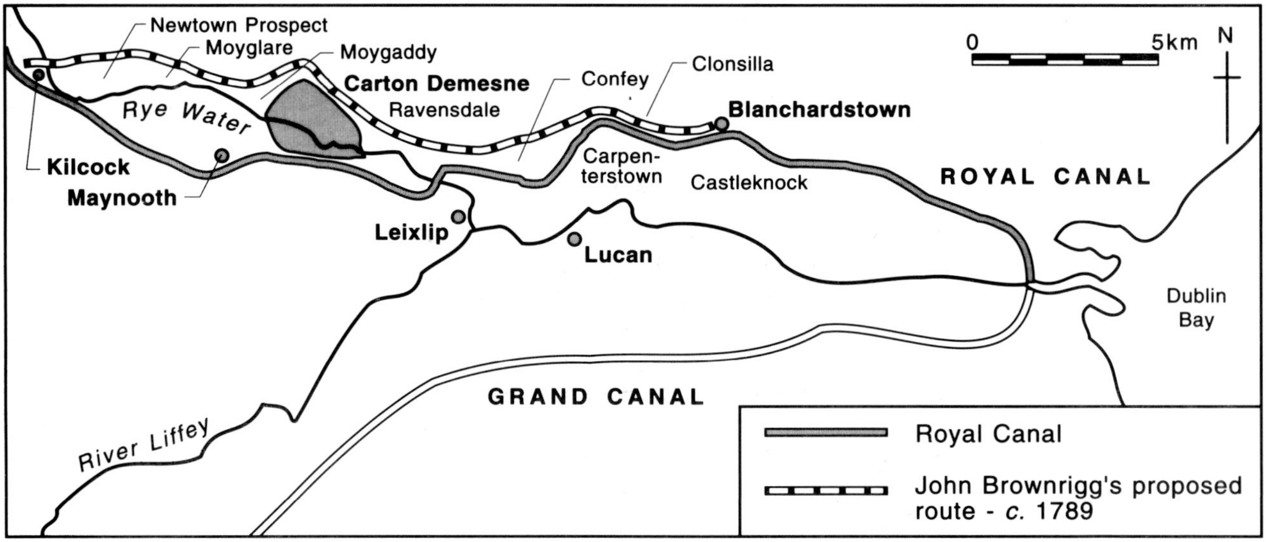

Figure 5: Approximate plan of John Brownrigg's proposed route c.1789, from Dublin to Kilcock, co. Kildare.

the river, the line passed two ravines, one at a place called the Island and the other called Shaughlins Glyn, and then proceeded to the cross-roads at Ravensdale. With Ravensdale on the right and Carton Demesne on the left, the line continued outside the walls of the estate.

The line proposed for the canal continued north of Moygaddy over some very uneven ground with the option of acquiring water to feed the canal from three streams in this area. From this point it was proposed to continue to Moyglare and again, an ample supply of water was available from two more streams which were to be used as feeders. Passing to the north of the church at Moyglare the line continued through very favourable ground to Newtown Prospect and from there to the town of Kilcock, twenty miles from Dublin (Fig. 5).

After passing Kilcock the ground for three miles comprised an even, regular, inclined plain mostly in meadow. In this area Brownrigg intended to have three single locks, one at the Bridge of Kilcock and the upper lock of the three at the high road at the Ford of Oldtown. He next proposed the commencement of a long level which extended for about sixteen miles, past the Bog of Cappagh and over the Blackwater river to Moyvalley. He proposed to level around the south edge of Cappagh Bog rather than make a cut right through the middle of it as this required little or no drainage. It was Brownrigg's intention to cut the canal to a level that would bring him over the Blackwater with an aqueduct about twenty feet above the surface of the river. He levelled from Cloncurry to the Blackwater but at some stage later advised the company not to use this line, saying that "Although it may be the shortest it will certainly be the dearest". He recommended instead that they should keep on the south side of Captain Ford's house at Johnstown, then cross the Blackwater river above Johnstown Bridge and turn along the western side of the river until this line joined the original line at Kilmore. By these changes the levels of sinking at Johnstown and Newcastle would be greatly reduced and it would also be possible to pick up two considerable brooks, one of which turned a mill.

From Moyvalley to Kinnegad, Brownrigg levelled three routes, the first by Garrister, another through Clonard which passed over the Boyne river at Mulphedder and on towards Kinnegad by an aqueduct, and a third route by Ashfield and Kilwarden. The last was the line which Brownrigg preferred as it was the cheapest and greatly shortened the main line to county Westmeath. It had better ground for crossing the Kinnegad river, was approximately one mile shorter, had lower embankments and did not require an aqueduct to enter the town of Kinnegad.

From Kinnegad, Brownrigg proceeded through the Bog of Downs to Rathconnell, keeping Rathwire on his right. He intended to make the summit level of the canal in the Bog of Downs, at the same level as the surface of Lough Owel, in order that the lake might feed directly into the canal at its summit (Fig. 6). This would have meant a thirty-five foot sinking in the bog for a length of one and a quarter miles, with a summit level six and a half miles in length including the branch to Lough Owel, for a water supply, and another to Mullingar.

Brownrigg's instructions from the company were to find the most direct route from Dublin to the river Shannon and he believed that this could be best achieved by proceeding via flat ground in the neighbourhood of Ballinaleck. With this in mind he left Mullingar off the main route one and a half miles to the left and proceeded

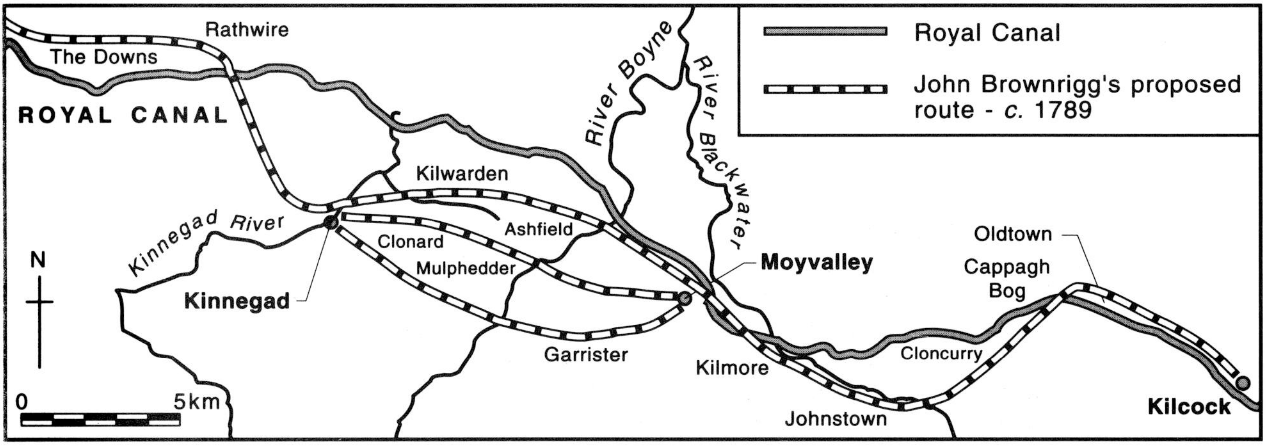

Figure 6: Approximate plan of John Brownrigg's proposed route c.1789, from Kilcock, co. Kildare, to The Downs, co. Westmeath.

by the foot of Knockdrin where in a distance of about half-a-mile he found himself in the valley through which the river Gaine flowed with a descent of eighty feet to a level of ninety-six feet below Lough Owel. From near the summit level, he followed this vale of flat ground to Multyfarnham and then on until the river Gaine turned into Lough Derravaragh. As the last part of this route was unsuitable, he tried a new one branching off at Multyfarnham via flat ground which led him by Ballyharney to the river Inny. At this point, he proposed to cross into the lands of Cappagh by an aqueduct and then he hoped to cross through county Longford towards Longford town and the Shannon. He tried two lines westward from Edgeworthstown, by Lisfarrell and by Ardagh but on each of these routes the ground was too high and would have necessitated a second summit level.

It was now November and it had rained almost continuously, but Brownrigg was determined not to give up. Given the difficulties he had encountered, he felt satisfied that with his knowledge of the country and its rivers, he could find a way of running the line on a more southerly route from Ballyharney by the Inny to Tennelick and from there to Keenagh and Killashee. At this point, he finally began to descend towards the Shannon through the Bog of Gowlan. From here, he proposed to turn the main trunk of the canal towards Longford town and to make a branch to Cloondara on the Shannon. This would have made the length of the canal from the North Wall in Dublin to Cloondara a total distance of ninety-six miles (Fig. 7).

On completion of his survey, Brownrigg returned to Dublin where many suggestions were made as to how the line could be shortened and improved. Particular suggestions came from Lord Sunderlin and Sir Robert Hudson at whose desire an order was made to have a new survey carried out to see if the main line of the canal could be carried through Mullingar and also on a more southerly route from Kinnegad towards Mullingar. This survey was never undertaken as Brownrigg's time was occupied with making maps and marking out the ground for the new works.[27]

The Charter of the Royal Canal

The subscription list for the Royal Canal closed on Friday 8 October 1789. £10,000 was offered over and above the £134,000 required but the additional money was rejected.[28] The Company's Charter was enrolled on 24

Figure 7: Approximate plan of John Brownrigg's proposed route c.1789, fro Mullingar to Cloondara, co. Longford.

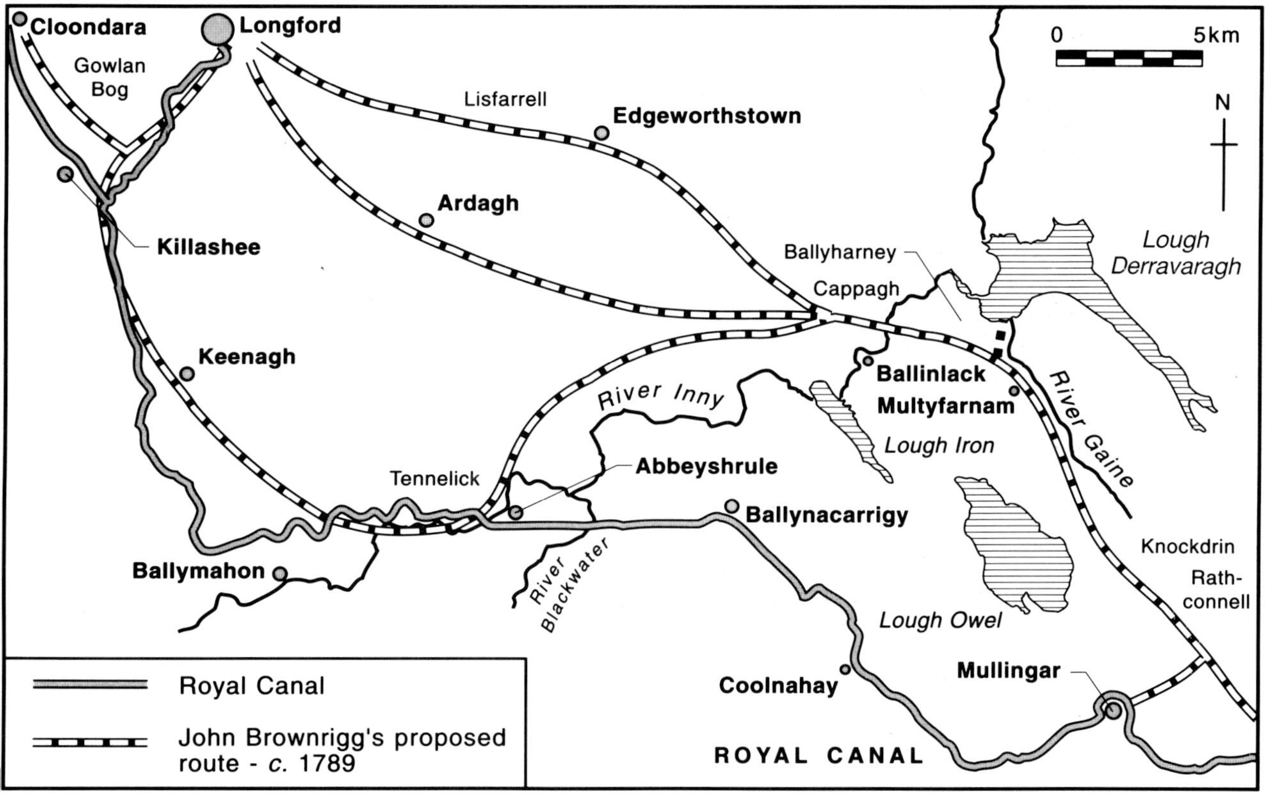

October 1789 and set out the rules and regulations to be observed. The route described was similar to that in the first petition to parliament, the results of Brownrigg's detailed survey not yet being available. The canal was to start at the new Custom House and to terminate at Tarmonbarry in county Longford. It was to pass through or near Kilcock, Kinnegad and Mullingar. If they so wished "they could make branches to Trim, Kells, Athboy and Castletowndelvin or any other towns or places that seemed expedient". A branch from the main line was to be constructed to connect into a harbour at Bolton Street and the junction of Domnick Street in Dublin.

As previously described, the parliamentary grant of £66,000 together with the £134,000 subscriptions made up the capital stock of the company. If required the company had the power to increase the subscription to £300,000 if difficulties arose. No subscription was to be less than £100 nor greater than £5,000, in order to avoid a monopoly by any one person; those acquiring more than the said £5,000 of capital stock would have to forfeit the extra shares to the company to be disposed of by them at public auction. For a shareholder to be entitled to vote at a company meeting, the minimum number of shares required was three. Of the one hundred and thirty-four subscribers listed, only four subscribed less than £300, each of the said four putting up £100 each. The company was to receive a rate not exceeding 3d a mile for every ton weight of cargo and 2d per mile for every passenger. An additional 2d per ton was to be charged for every lock that a vessel passed through between the junction of Phibsborough Road and the river Liffey. The tolls charged on corn and meal brought to Dublin were not to exceed 1½d per ton per mile.

On Friday 13 November the subscribers met at the company boardroom in Dawson Street and elected forty-one directors to oversee the business of the company[29] for the following twelve months. On the following day, the new directors elected the following officers to run the day-to-day business of the canal: Treasurer – Sir William Gleadowe Newcomen; Secretary

– Richard Gladwell; Accountant – John Savage and Law Agent – Richard Cudmore.

In November 1789, the company employed Richard Evans, an engineer who, at that time, was employed by the Grand Canal Company. Evans had experience of canal engineering having been in charge of the construction of the Barrow line for the latter company.[30] He was employed by the Royal Canal Company on a part-time basis, with a salary of £300 per annum.[31] One month after taking up this position, he was dismissed by the Grand Canal Company[32] presumably for taking up employment with a competitor. On 17 November 1789 Evans began to lay out and take levels on the proposed route between Dublin and Kilcock [33] As Brownrigg's survey was not completed until late November with no drawings being prepared until after that, it must be assumed that Evans attempted to lay out the initial parts of the canal without sections or any detailed knowledge of the proposed line. Following a similar route to Brownrigg's, he levelled north to the Rye Water by Ravensdale in the direction of Kilcock. Encountering an area of unfavourable ground, he then surveyed south of the river. The revised route brought the line through Maynooth and near Leixlip. This route meant that instead of the canal running on the relatively flat ground north of the Rye Water, it would now have to cross that river and the deep valley in which it flowed by means of an aqueduct. The Carpenterstown quarry was once again encountered and Evans estimated that at least a mile of sinking would be required there.

Estimates were prepared for both of Evans's routes: the south line via Castleknock, which incorporated the quarry he estimated would cost £39,409-0-10½, while the north route via Blanchardstown and Ravensdale was costed at £36,615-11-2½. Despite the higher cost and Evans's advice, the company chose the southern route. On 3 March 1791[34] he was instructed to lay out the line through Castleknock and then via Maynooth to Kilcock. As will be seen later, this decision was to have an adverse effect on the building of the canal and devastating effects on the finances of the canal company.

In February 1790 the company presented a bill to parliament[35] to alter the route of the canal from that described in the Charter. The "Act for better enabling the Royal Canal Company to carry on and complete the Royal Canal from the city of Dublin to Tarmonbarry on the river Shannon" cites two alterations on the route. The first was of little significance: the branch line which was to start at Prospect and terminate at Bolton Street would now terminate at Broadstone instead. This change was made because local residents were opposed to this section of the line.[36] The second and more fundamental change concerned the diversion of the canal through the town of Maynooth. This was the first occasion that it was suggested that the canal should run through the village.

No explanation is offered in the company's bill as to why Maynooth was now to be included on the route. Over the years, it has been suggested that the diversion was at the instigation of the Duke of Leinster who owned the

Figure 8: The Duke of Leinster's private harbour at Maynooth, co. Kildare.

village and who was a director of the canal company. In 1739, he returned to Maynooth to live at Carton House.[37] He rebuilt the house and created the great wall which surrounds it. In 1756, he began replanning and rebuilding the village, a project which took over forty years to complete. It would, therefore, be reasonable to assume that he would want the new waterway to pass through his new village.

A small stone harbour in the canal bank, directly opposite the side entrance gate to Carton Demesne, was recently discovered during renovations. The siting of this private harbour would suggest that the Duke of Leinster had more influence in the Royal Canal Company than many of the other directors. While no evidence exists to prove the Duke's involvement in the diversion of the line, it would be a reasonable assumption that it was done at his request.

Chapter Three

The Construction of the Royal Canal

The Royal Canal was constructed between 1790 and 1817. A five mile branch from one mile south-east of Killashee to Longford town was commenced in 1827 and completed in 1831. The main trunk line was built in two stages. The first stage between Dublin city and Coolnahay in county Westmeath (59.7 miles from Dublin and 5.62 miles beyond Mullingar) was built by the Royal Canal Company. This company was dissolved by an Act of Parliament in 1813 when it was decided that it was no longer in a position to complete the canal. The second stage from Coolnahay to Cloondara in county Longford was built by the Directors General of Inland Navigation.

Phase one of the canal from Dublin to Coolnahay was the most difficult section to construct. Problems with the construction including inadequate supervision of work and with the chosen route drained the financial resources of the company. In contrast, few problems were experienced with the second phase from Coolnahay to Cloondara and it was completed successfully in three years.

From the Liffey to Kilcock

In the twenty mile stretch between Dublin and Kilcock, major difficulties were encountered. To complicate matters, bad workmanship and incorrect levels were common on the line between Dublin and Ashtown and these incurred additional unnecessary expense. The limestone quarry at Carpenterstown, which should have been avoided, was more difficult to excavate than

Figure 9:
The 5th lock (Westmoreland Lock) at Cross Guns Bridge, Phibsborough.

anticipated and became extremely expensive to complete. The decision to route the canal via Maynooth which necessitated the building of an aqueduct over the Rye Water near Leixlip was another of the elements on this stretch which caused the company to become bankrupt by 1794.

The first section of canal to be built was that between the river Liffey and Ashtown in county Dublin. Work began in late April or early May 1790.[1] The digging started at the site of the intersection of the Broadstone branch with the main line at Prospect close to Phibsborough Road (Cross Guns Bridge) and proceeded simultaneously in a westerly direction towards Ashtown and eastwards towards the river Liffey. Ten locks were built on this four-mile stretch by contractors at a predetermined price. The work proceeded very well at first. Labourers were paid ten pence per day; however, after a dispute with the company in June this rate was increased to eighteen pence per day. By November the company was ready to commence building the first lock at Cross Guns (now the 5th lock). The ceremony for laying the first stone was performed on Thursday 12 November by John Fane, Earl of Westmoreland. The ceremony attracted such a large crowd that it was necessary for soldiers to keep them back. The Earl was presented with an inscribed silver trowel to mark the occasion and in return he presented twenty guineas to Richard Evans to be distributed among the workmen.

The workmanship on this section, particularly on the locks and bridges, was of a very poor standard. From 1790 until September 1792, the work proceeded without a full-time engineer: although Richard Evans was in charge theoretically, he spent very little time at the Royal Canal, the major portion of his time being spent working on the Boyne Navigation near Navan in county Meath where he was also employed as engineer.[2] Work on the Royal Canal was carried out mainly under the direction of supervisors appointed by Evans before construction began.[3] These supervisors were negligent and failed to identify problems with the construction of the bridges and lock chambers at an early enough stage to have the faults rectified before the work was complete. Thus several bridges and locks had to be demolished and rebuilt while others needed extensive remedial work. Newcomen Bridge on the Summerhill Road collapsed when it was almost complete because of insufficient bonding of the stone work and four workmen were killed in the incident.[4] Westmoreland Lock at Phibsborough Road had to be partly demolished and rebuilt and the 7th lock at Cabra was fitted with sluice frames which had begun to rot prior to being fitted.

Frequently, the contracts overran the agreed price and additional money was claimed for completing or rectifying work.[5] In many cases the company had no option but to pay as the specification was shown to be inadequate in describing the size and quality of materials needed. The lack of information contained in the specifications was the fault of Evans who was a company employee. It indicates the enormous pressure he was under in trying to service both the Royal Canal and the Boyne Navigation. Incorrect levels and the misplacing of locks added further complications and suggest that by 1793, this section of the work was in total chaos.

While it is true that the supervisors failed in their duties by allowing sub-standard work to continue, overall responsibility for this state of affairs must be attributed to the directors of the company. They should have appointed a Chief Engineer and a Resident Assistant Engineer at the start of construction, as was customary in the English system of canal building.[6] The Assistant Engineer would have been responsible for co-ordinating work on the various sections of the canal. Under his direction, supervisors would have taken charge of specific areas such as masonry and would have had to report to him as the work proceeded. A failure to have such a structured organisation meant that the canal was being built in an unco-ordinated manner and without direction. The money saved on salaries by not appointing suitable engineering staff was very little in comparison with what was being spent rectifying the problems of unsupervised work.

The Docks, the Quarry and the Aqueduct

Two of the largest obstacles encountered on the Dublin to Kilcock section of the canal were Carpenterstown Quarry and the Rye Water aqueduct. In addition to these and other problems associated with construction, the company were also building the docks at the river Liffey near the North Wall.

In April 1791[7] the company applied to parliament for increased funds to build extended docks at the river Liffey. These were to be capable of holding up to two hundred ships at any one time. Graving docks were also to be constructed in order to facilitate repairs and the building of new vessels. It was acknowledged that since the previous applications of April 1789 costs had increased and therefore that an additional sum of money, £23,000, was needed now to carry out the work. It was hoped that £7,000 would be paid immediately and the balance be paid when the work was completed in three years time. Like the previous petitions, this one was successful.[8] Work commenced on the new docks on 1 March 1792.[9]

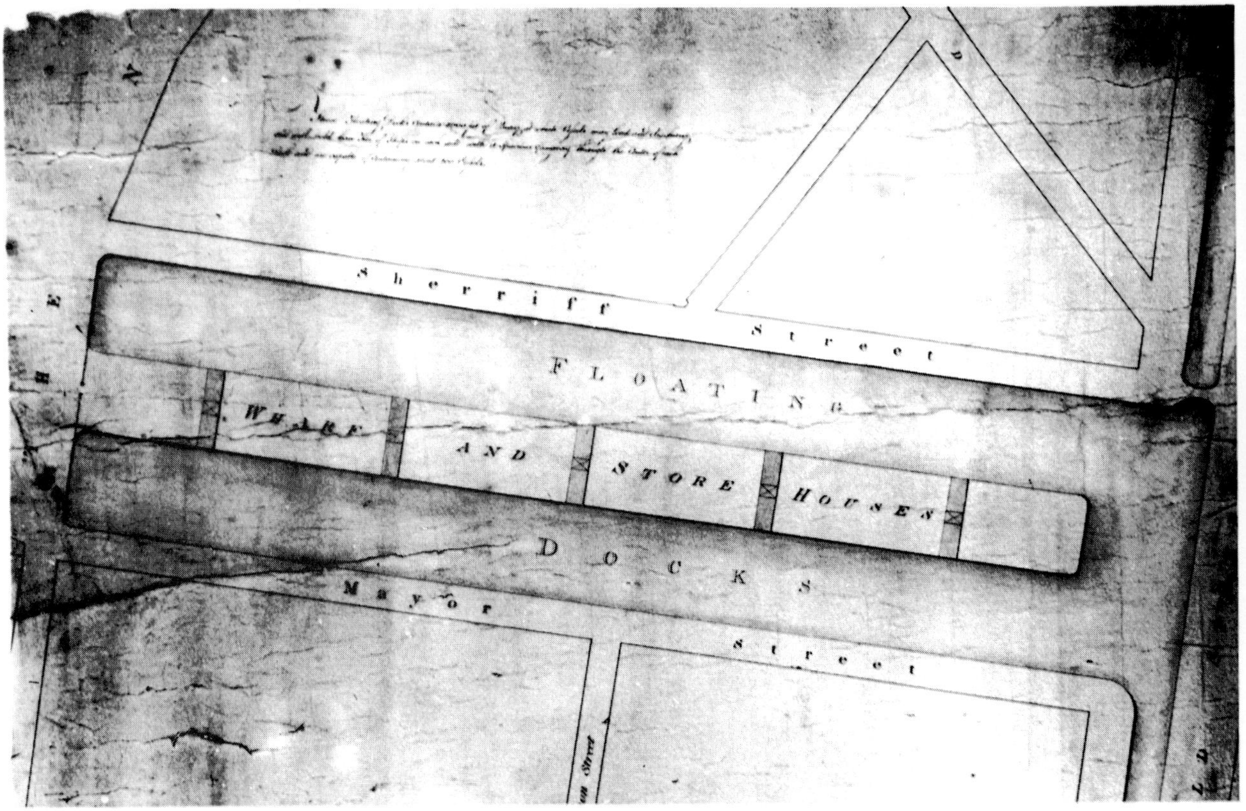

Figure 10: Plan of the proposed docks at the river Liffey by William Jessop, c.1789. (City of Dublin Archive)

The routing of the main line of the canal via Maynooth necessitated the building of the Rye aqueduct to carry the canal one hundred feet above the Rye Water near Leixlip. The aqueduct was designed by Richard Evans who estimated that it would cost £8,449-4-0 to construct.[10] This price did not include the cost of making it waterproof. His estimate was close to that of Thomas Keary of Kilcock, county Kildare, who tendered in July 1791 to build the aqueduct at a cost of £8,950.[11] Keary's tender was rejected by the company. Instead, they embarked on a cost-cutting exercise and in November 1791 they began excavating and building the foundations of the proposed aqueduct using their own workforce. As with many of the other masonry works on this section, the workmanship was faulty. Although a contract was made for £7,500 with the Dublin building firm of Bergin and Semple in February 1792 to complete the aqueduct from above ground level, that firm was unable to complete it due to the collapsing of the foundations in 1792 and again in 1793. The aqueduct was not completed until 1795; the final cost was £28,230-18-5[12] more than three times the original estimate. The arch and retaining walls which span

Figure 11:
(top) Looking east along the Rye Aqueduct, near Leixlip.
(bottom) The Rye Water flowing one hundred feet below, as viewed from the Rye Aqueduct.

the Rye Water required 7,652 perches of masonry, and 150,000 cubic yards of earth was used in the embankments.

Much of the excavation of the canal from Dublin to Kilcock was completed roughly by 1792 with the exception of the mile and a half through Carpenterstown Quarry. Excavation began here in July 1791. The cost of excavating and completing the Carpenterstown section was estimated by Evans at £10,223-12-0. Once again, this was an underestimate: the final cost of carrying the canal through Carpenterstown was £41,968-5-1[13] of which approximately £10,000 was spent on gunpowder and equipment. In the initial stages of the work quarrymen were paid between 1s 6d and 2s 2d per cubic yard of rock removed; by the time they reached the end of the digging the rate had increased to 3s 4d. Tools were supplied for the work and a plot of ground where they could erect a cabin was also supplied.

In April 1792 at the request of the company, the English engineer Sir Thomas Hyde Page arrived in Ireland to advise and act as consultant to the canal.[14] His arrival suggests that the directors had now become aware of the major difficulties which had arisen. It indicates also that they were now aware that it would be impossible for Evans to continue alone and in his part-time capacity.

On Page's inspection of the line between Dublin and Lough Owel with Richard Evans, it was agreed that it was well laid out as far as the river Boyne in county Meath. However, after his visit to Mullingar, Page disagreed with Brownrigg's proposal that the town should be connected by a branch and suggested that the main line should run through the town.[15]

Page carried out no in-depth survey of the proposed line of the canal other than this cursory inspection to Mullingar. It would appear that most of his time was spent surveying and advising on the dock at the North Wall.

Page returned to Dublin in May 1793 when he acted as consultant to a committee of prominent company directors, which had been set up to examine the appointment of various officers employed on the work and their respective duties.[16] With this committee, he was to advise on how the work could progress in a more satisfactory manner and was also to suggest improvements to the proposed route. In July 1793, the committee reported on its findings. The poor standard of workmanship described earlier was the focal point of their report. The opinion was expressed that it was the engineer's negligence which had caused several of the works to be so imperfectly constructed. Very few of the terms of a number of the relevant contracts had been complied with. The report claimed also that the company had received no monthly or quarterly reports from the engineer or from other officers and therefore that there was complete ignorance as to the progress of the works. Money had been spent in a lavish and shameful way. It was recommended that the engineer's salary be stopped until he gave a satisfactory explanation as to what had caused the problems.

An audit of the company's accounts revealed that the problems encountered with the building of the canal had seriously eroded the company's finances. As stated previously, the estimate to complete the canal to the river Shannon was for £197,098. The actual expenditure on the works from May 1790 to June 1793 amounted to £118,148-11-5 by which time the canal was only partly completed to Kilcock. The significance of this situation was that instead of the capital stock of the company being used to build a navigation to the Shannon, the principal part was being used to complete the line from Dublin to Kilcock.

A notable feature of Page's report was that no blame was placed on the directors themselves who were of course ultimately responsible for the administration of the complete project. No explanation is given as to why, after three years, no progress reports were being submitted to the directors nor why expenditure had risen so high without this being noticed by the accountant or his fellow directors. It is perhaps not surprising that the engineer alone was blamed as the investigating committee was comprised of company directors.

One result of the setting up of the investigation was that a bitter feud erupted between Evans and Brownrigg. Both presented submissions to the committee, each attempting to avoid taking responsibility for all that had gone wrong. These submissions show the role each had in the construction of this part of the line. Brownrigg, admitting that it was possible to make mistakes in the levels he had taken, emphasised that such mistakes could normally be spotted by the engineer during construction and rectified. Evans freely admitted to being frequently absent from the workings due to his commitments elsewhere, but placed all of the blame for the problems encountered on Brownrigg's levels and sections.

An examination of both men's submissions and of the committee's report[17] shows clearly that neither Brownrigg nor Evans were totally to blame for the problems the company had at this time, even allowing for Brownrigg's mistakes and Evans's absences. The main difficulty was that construction was progressing without the direction of a full-time engineer. This was the responsibility of the directors, not Evans: the directors, being well aware of Evans's absences, still allowed the work to be carried on under the direction of supervisors, and at the same time, allowed their own orders to be disobeyed with regard to the submission of progress reports.

The committee, having considered the reports of Evans and Brownrigg, completely exonerated Brownrigg of all blame. It was recommended that Evans be dismissed along with the supervisors of masonry and earthworks. Although Evans was blamed for all that had gone wrong, the recommendation of the committee concerning him was not implemented. Evans continued to work for the company as engineer on the canal until his death in January 1802. Why Evans continued to be employed is not known.

Although the committee exonerated Brownrigg of all blame, this was not the view taken by John Binns. It was

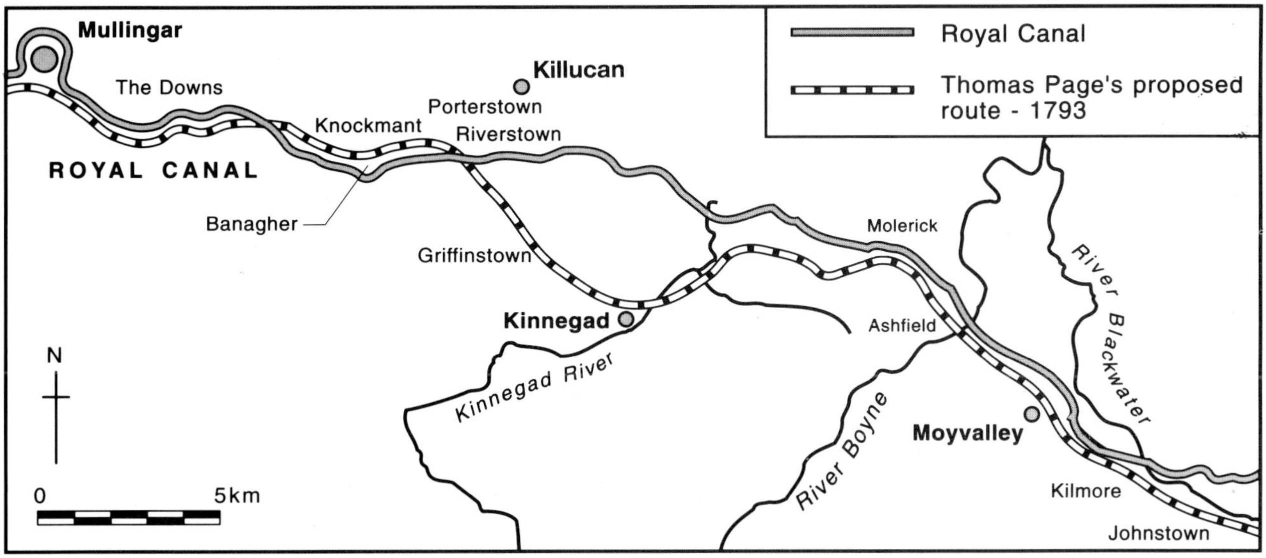

Figure 12: Approximate plan of Thomas Page's proposed route, 1793, from Johnstown to Mullingar.

his private opinion that Brownrigg was responsible for the problems and not Evans and he made every effort to prevent Brownrigg from being paid[18] for the work he had undertaken. In view of the powerful influence Binns had in the company it is likely that Evans was retained as engineer at his request.

During the summer of 1793, Page made a new and complete survey of the proposed line from Kilcock to Longford.[19] Beyond Johnstown, county Meath, he recommended that the main line should run south of Brownrigg's route to Moyvalley and thence north through Ashfield which was situated on Brownrigg's favoured route. From here, his line proceeded to Molerick and then to Kinnegad where a harbour would be built. The line then passed through the town parks on favourable ground and on through the cut-away bogs and bottoms of Griffinstown, Riverstown and Porterstown where a deep sinking of twenty-six feet would be needed. Here it was intended to use a stream coming from White Lake as a feeder. From here the route proposed by Page passed through the townlands of Banagher and Knockmant to the main Dublin road to Mullingar which was encountered at The Downs about thirty-seven miles from Dublin (Fig. 12).

Page was critical of Brownrigg's proposed line at the summit level. Here, he suggested that instead of carrying the main line from Rathconnell Bridge south of Knockarin and on towards the river Gaine with a branch

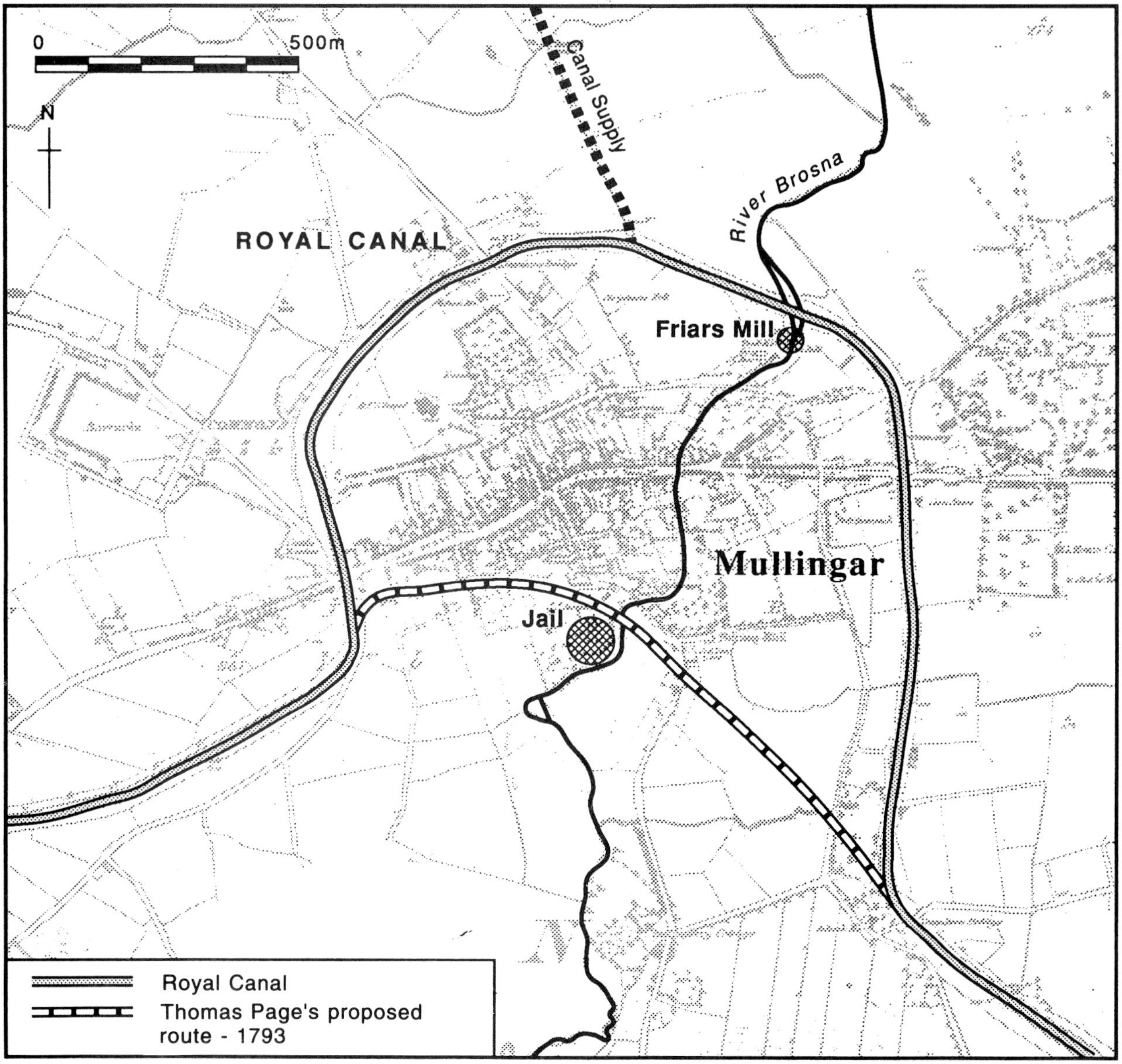

Figure 13: Approximate plan of Thomas Page's proposed route, 1793, through the town of Mullingar.

from Rathconnell Bridge to Mullingar the canal should pass south of Lough Owel and through the town of Mullingar itself. A perceived advantage of taking the main line through Mullingar was to benefit from the business which could be generated by the meeting in Mullingar of the roads from Athlone, Ballymahon and Longford.

Accordingly, Page's line continued onwards from the Downs to Baltrasna. After passing Plodstown and the mill at Ballinderry, this line involved falling to low ground in the town parks and gardens of Mullingar. The canal would pass to the south side of the town where it would traverse low meadows and gardens and cross the river Brosna at about thirty feet above river level. It would then cross the lower street between the jail and the market place and continue to the western side of the town. The main problem with this route was that it would have required the construction of a huge embankment and bridge over the lower street with the demolition of houses on each side in order to enable an approach road to be built. A feeder from Lough Owel was to join the canal at the western side of the town (Fig. 13).

Page's route continued from Mullingar to Coolnahay and from here through Ballynacarrigy to Tinnalick which entailed crossing the river Inny with an aqueduct. He levelled from here to Longford but gives no details of the precise route in his report. He does, however, state that he was in agreement with Brownrigg's route and levels of 1789.

Page had no further involvement with the Royal Canal Company after 1793. His recommendations with regard to changes in the route were accepted by the company. However as will be seen later only some were implemented. Rather, as the engineering personnel changed so too did the route in accordance with their own ideas.

Difficulties with the Financing

The canal which had only been partially completed from Dublin to Kilcock had cost £118,148-11-5 up to June 1793.[20] Thus the estimate provided in 1789 to construct the canal had only covered the construction of approximately twenty miles of work. One of the greatest problems the company had from this point on was a lack of working capital. Several attempts to raise money from parliament and the subscribers helped to complete the line to Newcastle, county Meath, twenty-eight miles from Dublin by 1800.

On 10 July 1793, the board of directors of the company decided to discontinue the work on the dock at the North Wall until the canal reached Mullingar.[21] During their investigation into their problems, it was discovered that there would not be an ample supply of water to feed the canal and the docks until Lough Owel was reached. Parliament was advised that discontinuance of the work on the Liffey docks was a temporary measure and that it was intended that the work would resume when funds were available. The £7,000 which had been advanced for the work would be returned subsequently.

The inability of the company to refund the £7,000 speedily to the exchequer caused the first parliamentary enquiry into the company's affairs. A committee[22] set up to carry out the investigation established the same reasons for the company's difficulties as had been revealed by its own investigation.

In order for the company to continue constructing the line between Dublin and Kilcock, it was necessary to raise £9,800 by subscriptions in 1794, and an additional £40,300 the following year. When the canal was completed to Kilcock in 1796[23] the company petitioned parliament for a further £50,000 financial assistance. In addition to this £50,000 they intended to raise another £100,000 by issuing more stock. These new monies would allow completion of the canal to Coolnahay, the end of the summit level, six miles beyond Mullingar. The intended route from Kilcock specified in the company's 1796 petition was through Thomastown or Kinnegad to Mullingar and to Coolnahay. While parliament agreed[24] to grant the money, it did reserve it until February 1798 when a statute[25] was passed granting £25,000 only and then on the condition that the company must complete the canal as far as Thomastown, county Westmeath without seeking further financial aid.

During the two years' delay awaiting the passing of this statute, work continued on the canal. To enable the completion of the four-mile stretch from Kilcock to Cloncurry, a further £10,000 was raised by issuing further stock. In 1799, a further sum of £28,000 was raised by the same method. By 1800, the canal had reached Newcastle, county Meath, twenty-eight miles west of Dublin.

Directors General of Inland Navigation

By the end of the eighteenth century, the debentures scheme set up in 1788[26] to encourage the development of inland navigation had come under scrutiny. A parliamentary inquiry into the scheme in 1800[27] resulted in responsibility for the government financing of inland navigation being placed in the hands of a new body known as the Directors General of Inland Navigation. The sum of £500,000 was made available to the directors to spend on navigation works as they saw fit.[28]

The possibility of a new revenue source brought hope to the Royal Canal Company at a time when it looked certain that it would be unable to complete the canal with its own financial resources. The twenty-eight miles from Dublin to Newcastle had cost £350,000 and the docks at the Liffey and Broadstone Harbour were still incomplete.[29]

Seizing the opportunity to dispose of any further financial problems, the company made a proposal to the Directors General that the canal should be completed totally at public expense. However, the directors of the canal company wished to retain full control of its management. Not surprisingly, the proposal drew a sharp reaction from the Directors General who were quick to point out that £25,000 had been granted by parliament in February 1798, to enable the company to complete to Thomastown on the condition that no further aid would be sought until this point had been reached.[30] While totally rejecting the idea of funding the completion of the entire works, the Directors General did agree to a compromise whereby they would provide the sum of £95,866 to carry on the work to the end of the summit level at Coolnahay and complete the docks at Dublin and any other outstanding work. Although this arrangement provided a short-term solution to the company's problem it was not without conditions; the company was forced to reduce its existing tolls and to keep these at the reduced level until the canal reached the Shannon.

While in theory the canal company was still under the control of its own directors, the Directors General of Inland Navigation had a considerable input into its affairs from this point on. Surveys and inspections were carried out frequently by them on the sections of canal under construction and accounts were closely monitored. The Directors General also carried out surveys to establish alternative routes to those proposed by the company.

Brownrigg's Survey 1801

To establish the condition of the canal prior to funds being allocated, the Directors General instructed John Brownrigg on 5 February 1801 to carry out a survey of the existing canal and of the line proposed by Page in 1793[31] as far as Coolnahay, county Westmeath, the end of the summit level. While Brownrigg was only acting as a consultant for the directors, he suggested substantial changes to Page's proposed route which were later implemented by the company. Brownrigg's report describes clearly the condition of the canal from the North Wall to where it was dammed at the river Blackwater a quarter of a mile beyond Newcastle. While he did not explicitly criticise the line, most of which did not follow the route he suggested in 1789, there is a strong suggestion in the report of his disapproval of it.

His analysis of the proposed line from the Blackwater to Coolnahay shows clearly that no lessons had been learned from the company's previous experience in choosing its route. He remarked that the line chosen from the Blackwater to one and a half miles beyond the Boyne "was as bad and expensive as can be imagined". About a mile of this section was laid out from Moyvalley through Ashfield to Molerick from where Page's line continued towards Kinnegad. Brownrigg recommended that this section be changed and suggested that the line should pass through Ballynabarny to Blackshade bridge and on to Molerick where it rejoined the lock-spitted section.

The proposed section of canal from Molerick to the town of Kinnegad as suggested by Page in 1793 was impracticable in Brownrigg's opinion. After taking levels, he found the ground in the first mile to be very low and to run a canal through it would therefore be very expensive. It would also have been necessary to have two very long, high embankments over the Kinnegad and Kilwarden rivers in order to enable the town to be reached. Page's line continued to Kinnegad where a harbour was to be built.

Brownrigg felt that Kinnegad could be served equally well by running a branch from the main line to the town. In any case the town was only eight miles from the Grand Canal at Edenderry and little trade could be expected because of this. The road north-west from Kinnegad towards county Longford might in the short term bring considerable trade to the Royal Canal, but this road came from Mullingar to which it was intended to continue the line of the canal anyway. There would be an enormous saving in expense by not running the main line through Kinnegad as the branch line would require only a small tunnel or aqueduct. Brownrigg's preference was to have the main line continue from Molerick towards Mullingar via Thomastown. Although no details are given in his report of any survey taking place between Molerick and Thomastown it is possible that he did investigate the possibility of running a line between these two centres. It is also probable that he made strong recommendations to the Directors General that this route should be adopted although this is not recorded in his report.

The planned line of the canal from the townland of Banagher, county Westmeath, to Mullingar as envisaged by Page was to continue through the Downs on ground which presented no difficulties for about two and a half miles. After passing this area, Brownrigg anticipated that the work would become expensive due to high ground at Baltrasna. This was to be the beginning of the summit

Figure 14: The Royal Canal passing through Cappagh Bog.

level, but it would require a deep sinking of thirty feet for about three miles in a variety of terrain. Brownrigg advised that the company reconsider before undertaking this work and favoured an alternative route from the Bog of Downs to Rathconnell Bog which was part of the original line chosen by him in 1789. Yet, the directors chose the former line suggested by Page via Kinnegad and Baltrasna.

The anxiety on the part of the directors not to pass through Rathconnell Bog related to difficulties which had been encountered already while traversing Cappagh Bog, three miles beyond Kilcock. This was described by Brownrigg as "the worst kind imaginable". It consisted of a soft fungus fed by a lake at its centre. Although drains had been laid some years previously, it was still in a semi-fluid state when construction of the canal began. Because of the difficulties experienced here, the directors were prepared to risk the expense of cutting deep sinkings through rock, if necessary, to avoid all bogs encountered thereafter.

On examining the Rathconnell Bog however, Brownrigg discovered that unlike Cappagh Bog, this area had responded favourably to drains which had been laid about seven years previously in anticipation of the arrival of the canal. When this area was first surveyed by him in 1789, he had found it to be extremely wet and soft but as a result of the drainage, the bog had consolidated and was considerably lower. Furthermore, the area had now begun to be populated with a number of small dwellings being erected. The area around the centre drain had been made into fields with potatoes, rye and rape growing in a number of places. A close inspection showed that the bog had sunk up to ten feet in places and that it was likely that the canal could be constructed through gravel which lay under the bog for practically the whole length of this line. This in Brownrigg's opinion was the best type of ground in which to build a canal.

Coming to Mullingar town, Brownrigg's idea was to abandon Page's route and to run the line around the east and north of the town crossing the turnpike road and then the river Brosna above Friars Mill where the valley was less than half as deep as it was on the south side of the town. The revised route would join Page's line on the western side of Mullingar having in effect formed a loop around the town. This was the route adopted by the Royal Canal Company when the canal reached the town in 1806 (Fig. 13).

Page's intended line from Mullingar to Coolnahay posed no real problems in Brownrigg's opinion, although it might require some deep sinking and embankments. It passed through arable land and some pasture, and several small streams along the route could be brought into the canal if they were required. By far the greatest advantage the canal would bring to this area would be to relieve the local scarcity of fuel.

From the Blackwater to Coolnahay

Although the company was ready to proceed with the line from Newcastle to Kinnegad along the route suggested by Page in 1793, legal difficulties arose which delayed the start of work. The legal advisers to the Directors General insisted that the line should run to Thomastown as specified in Statute 38 Geo. III c.79 and not to Kinnegad as the company proposed. After much debate between the company and the Directors General, it was agreed that the line could proceed to Kinnegad without requiring a new Act of Parliament. However the problem was not solved until November 1801.[32]

Again, when the company was poised to move forward with the work it suffered a further setback with the death of their engineer Richard Evans in January 1802.[33] To replace Evans, the company employed the English engineer John Rennie as Consultant and promoted Michael Sparks to Resident Engineer. Sparks was appointed an apprentice to Evans in 1792 when he was 23 years of age. Problems arose when, after surveying Page's proposed line, Rennie disagreed with the estimate arrived at by Evans. Evans had calculated that the aqueduct required to cross the river Boyne would cost £3,700 and that the masonry work onwards to Mullingar would cost £22,459-16-0.[34] Rennie revised both these figures bringing the cost of the aqueduct up to £12,000 and the masonry work to £35,946-1-7, thereby increasing the total cost by £21,786-5-7. Rennie estimated that all the work on this section would cost an additional £29,000-13-5.

Although considerable sections of the line from Molerick to Kinnegad were excavated. Rennie persuaded the company to abandon this line and to re-direct it through Thomastown, along the line favoured in 1801 by Brownrigg. His reasons for abandoning the Kinnegad line are not known but, as has been stated already, it was longer and thus more expensive than via Thomastown. The priority at this time was to reach Mullingar as quickly as possible and so the circuitous route through Kinnegad had presumably become unattractive. The company planned to return to the abandoned line at a later stage and to complete it as a branch to Kinnegad. However due to circumstances in the following years, this never occurred.

Plate 1:

(top left)
Land rack.
The rack is down and the sluice is closed.

(top right)
Part of the balance beam on a lock gate. The balance beam is used for opening and closing the lock gates.

(bottom)
Water flowing from a level into a lock chamber through a partly opened paddle in a lock gate.

The work from Molerick to Thomastown continued without much incident and it was expected that this section would be opened by 1 June 1805 and the section to Mullingar by 1 November 1805. While Thomastown was reached in October 1805, Mullingar was not reached until December 1806.[35] The delay in reaching Mullingar was caused by the need for a deep sinking near the town. In an attempt to reduce costs and to speed up the work, the company was forced to make this section a narrow channel, twenty-eight feet at the top and twenty-four feet at the bottom. The line was completed to the end of the summit level at Coolnahay seven miles west of Mullingar by the end of 1808. Although it was estimated in 1801 that it would cost £95,866-17-10 to complete the line from Thomastown to Coolnahay, the final cost amounted to £193,608-3-9.

Proposed Extensions to Lough Allen and Lough Erne

Although the ultimate destination of the canal from its inception was to be Tarmonbarry, several other lines for the western section were suggested from as early as 1807 and surveys were carried out on them. The company put forward a plan in 1807 to reduce the cost of construction by terminating the navigation at Lough Ree instead of Tarmonbarry.[36] The details of this plan are not known. It was more likely a suggestion rather than a plan and it is unlikely that a survey took place. This was not a practical solution for Lough Ree at that time was considered dangerous. Boats carrying timber, slate and farm produce were often stranded for up to three weeks on sand banks. Farmers sending corn to Dublin preferred to transport it fifteen miles by road to the Royal Canal at Coolnahay rather than risk boating it through Lough Ree and the Grand Canal.[37] John Rennie surveyed a line from Coolnahay to Ardagh and to Rooskey for the company in 1807 but exact details are not available.[38]

In 1809, John Killaly, engineer to the Directors General, carried out a major survey for them. His instruction was

Figure 15: John Killaly's proposed extensions to Royal Canal, 1809.

Plate 2: Views of Lough Owel near Mullingar, co. Westmeath, the main feeder for the Royal Canal.

Plate 3: (top) View from Kilpatrick Bridge, west of Mullingar, of the Royal Canal and the railway line which runs parallel to it from Dublin to just beyond Mullingar.
(bottom) The 25th lock at Footy's Bridge near Riverstown, co. Westmeath, before and after restoration.

to continue the canal in the most northerly direction that was feasible. Killaly proposed to terminate the canal at Coolnahay and to begin his new line by branching off at Thomastown, county Westmeath, and continue towards Castlepollard, Finae and Portanure and towards Lough Allen (Fig. 15). At Portanure a branch was to run towards Lough Erne. The total cost of this network of canals was estimated to be £520,000. To enable the canal to enter the Shannon, Killaly planned a ten and a half mile branch from Farthaman to Tarmonbarry at a cost of £83,600.

An accurate description of the country and of the potential trade on the routes proposed by Killaly was made by City Surveyor, Arthur Richard Neville for the company on the 18 June 1810.[39] The new line was to begin between the 20th and 21st locks and pass half a mile east of Killucan to Curristown. The ground in this area was very hilly with farming being divided equally between corn, meadow and pasture. On its east side, the canal would have large areas of bogland while on its west side, there would be small farms consisting of pasture and occasional fields of light oats until it reached Barbavilla. From here the route passed close to Lough Derravaragh through hilly ground comprising land planted with poor corn, with some pasture and on to within half a mile of Castlepollard. Again, the farms were small with a mixture of light oats and pasture. In Neville's opinion the tenantry seemed poor and no commercial advantage for the canal company would be gained in the area.

From Lough Derravaragh the line was to proceed by Coole and across the river Inny by Caldony. This area consisted of light pasture with some corn. From here the line continued to Portanure. Poor light pasture with some oats made up the bulk of the crops in this area and much of the land was low bog. After passing Portanure, the line continued, passing the river Erne on the east and Brucehill on the west. It continued on towards Killeshandra through a vale of rough pasture with some corn and tree plantations. The area around Killeshandra was hilly and set out in meadow and pasture, the corn grown in the area being of good quality. From here, the line proceeded towards the village of Milltown and on to Belturbet and Lough Erne.

The branch from Portanure to Lough Allen was to pass near the village of Scrabby and on to near Arvagh where there was a good corn mill and bleach green. On the west side of this line lay Lough Gowna, the east side being hilly pasture with very little tillage. En route to Ballinamuck the line would have passed through several bogs. The surrounding area comprised poor hilly land set in pasture. Few crops were grown and the roads were in very poor condition.

From Ballinamuck, the line was to continue towards the town of Mohill and from there to Bunnymore Bog, and to within a mile of the villages of Drumsna and Jamestown. From Jamestown the line was to proceed to Lough Allen passing near to the villages of Leitrim and Drumshanbo. The surrounding area consisted of very poor hilly pasture with scarcely enough land set in tillage to support the local inhabitants.

Neville's commission from the canal company was to survey the lines of the proposed extensions and to ascertain the nature of the countryside through which they would run and to evaluate the advantages they afforded. The total length of the extension from Thomastown to Lough Erne and Lough Allen was eighty-five miles. In Neville's opinion, the area to be served offered few advantages. There was a low population and the housing and the people were very poor. There existed no large farms on either side of the line for many miles. Only about one-third of the land was under tillage and the crops produced were generally poor. Few mills existed and sufficient water for them was available for less than half the year. Although it was reported that the area from Portanure to loughs Erne and Allen produced large quantities of butter, Neville found no evidence of this: there were no dairies recorded in his survey and he saw few cattle.

Neville did not make any recommendations as to whether the company should proceed with the line. To a certain extent, the exercise undertaken by him was academic for the cost of the proposed extensions was beyond the

Plate 4: The 12th lock at Blanchardstown, co. Dublin, before and after restoration.

financial resources of both the Directors General and the Royal Canal Company.

From Coolnahay to Tarmonbarry

While the foregoing proposed extensions are of interest, by far the most important work on the western section of the route after the initial surveys of Brownrigg and Page was carried out by Richard Evans at various times between 1790 and 1801. His proposed line was proceeded with from Coolnahay to Ballynacarrigy, where it was expected that a new linen industry would soon be in operation and many new houses had been built in the area ready for occupation by the workforce.

From Ballynacarrigy, the line was to proceed to near Tinnelick flour mills and across the river Inny to the village of Taghshinny and on to the villages of Kenagh, Killashee and Cloondara. The length from Coolnahay to Cloondara was twenty-four miles and no difficulties with construction were anticipated.

Neville also reported on this line and noted that it passed through an area of good tillage producing wheat, oats, potatoes and also some flax. The houses were of a better quality than those on Killaly's proposed northern route indicating a more prosperous population and there were fewer bogs, these being of a much smaller size. As in his report on the northerly route, Neville did not recommend that this route should be used. However, the more positive tone of his report suggested that this route was preferable.

The Royal Canal Company did not have the financial resources to continue the canal from Coolnahay to the Shannon. An appeal to the Directors General of Inland Navigation for further financial aid brought the several suggested lines under scrutiny. The shortest and cheapest route was preferred – that from Coolnahay to Cloondara.

The estimated cost of completing this extension was £306,525-15-11. The company was not in a position to meet this sum and so agreement was reached with the Directors General whereby the canal would be constructed for the time being onwards to Ballymahon only on the understanding that finance for the rest of the project would be raised later. The cost of this section was estimated at £106,638-1-3 of which £71,092-0-10 would be provided by the Directors General.

An appeal in 1811 by the Grand Canal Company to the Directors General against the Royal Canal extension to Ballymahon prevented the work from starting. The complaint was that the Royal Canal had from the beginning been an injury to the Grand Canal Company and an encroachment on their monopoly and that the proposed extension to Ballymahon would bring the line still closer to theirs while the reduced tolls being charged on the Royal Canal at the behest of the Directors General since 1801 would exacerbate the loss of business to the Grand Canal. The Grand Canal directors' biggest fear was that the Royal Canal would not continue on to Cloondara from Ballymahon at all but rather would seek to enter the river Inny and terminate in Lough Ree. As stated already, this was not in fact practical and was only considered briefly and rejected by the Royal Canal Company in 1807. If such an extension to Lough Ree had been built, it would have left the Royal Canal at a distance of only ten miles from Athlone, a town which was providing major business for the Grand Canal Company.

The Directors General considered the appeal of the Grand Canal Company but felt that no injury existed as the two canals were still twenty miles apart. However, on appeal to the Lord Lieutenant, the Grand Canal Company had the decision to grant money to the Royal Canal Company overturned. Thus the Ballymahon line was halted. As a result, the Royal Canal Company was forced to appeal to parliament to restore the funding but they were unsuccessful. Instead, an investigation by a House of Commons Committee was ordered and this resulted in the company being declared bankrupt. It was recommended that the company be dissolved.[40] Accordingly, in 1813, its property was vested in the

Directors General of Inland Navigation who were authorised in 1815 to complete the canal.[41]

A parliamentary enquiry[42] to investigate claims of the creditors of the company and to try to alleviate the hardship caused by the winding up of the company was carried out in 1815 and reported "that it was difficult to conclude how far the stockholders had been committed by the directors of the company and to what extent they were innocent sufferers because of the directors' mismanagement". However, it was recommended that on the formation of a new Royal Canal Company, all creditors and stockholders should be able to hold stock in the new company but that all directors of the old Royal Canal Company should be disbarred.

When the canal was completed in 1817, a new company was formed. The shareholders of the old company received £40 holding for every £100 of original stock.[43] While this sum may appear generous considering the company had been declared bankrupt in 1813, the offer was made because many of these shareholders were small investors who depended on dividends from their shares. From these stockholders a new board of directors was elected to run the company and the five Directors General, Daniel Corneille, Joshua Kemmis, Henry Paire, George Bouverie and John Armit,[44] were appointed as a Board of Control. They did not have power to dictate policy but they were to be fully informed on the state of the canal, proposed maintenance works and its financial position. All appointments, dismissals and legal matters, such as rents and leases, had to receive the board's approval.

The Directors General Complete the Line

With the Royal Canal Company dissolved, no time was wasted in the resumption of work. John Killaly, Engineer to the Directors General, carried out a survey of the proposed line from Coolnahay to Cloondara early in 1813.[45] This was a detailed survey accompanied by a map of the proposed line and a comprehensive estimate of the cost.

Killaly followed closely the line laid out by Evans. From Coolnahay to a mile and a half beyond Ballynacarrigy he followed the same course, but by inclining to the north from Rathkelet and crossing the river Inny at the Ford of Driminure, a long embankment over the Blackwater, a considerable length of deep sinking through Ballymagladdy Bog and several large embankments from there to Terlicken were avoided.

The route onwards to the Shannon was again similar to what was laid out already by Evans for much of its length, but by moving the positions of the locks and entering the Shannon through the Camlin river, the expense of an aqueduct was saved. Evans's line would have taken an estimated ten years to complete whereas with the alterations, Killaly proposed to complete it in four years at a cost of £198,110-5-4.

Killaly completed laying out his line from Coolnahay to Cloondara on 9 November 1813[46] and a contract was signed with the firm of Henry, Mullins and McMahon for work to commence on 27 May 1814, and to be completed by 1 March 1817.[47] Killaly had overall responsibility for the new works and reported directly to the Directors General. Unlike his predecessors, Killaly had a well structured team of engineers and supervisors working under him. Two resident engineers were appointed,[48] J. Alex Jones who had been employed as Resident Engineer for the Royal Canal Company from 1806, and Thomas Whitehead. There were six overseers: Charles Tarrant, Edward Cooke, John Killinger, Joseph Burke, William Musgrave and Hugh O'Neill. Jones was responsible for the works from Coolnahay to Ballymahon and Whitehead from there to the Shannon. The supervision of the work was increased further when on 29 July 1814, six assistant supervisors were appointed at £2 per week. One of those appointed was Michael Sparks who had succeeded Richard Evans as Resident Engineer on the canal after the latter's death in 1802.

J. Alex Jones never saw the completed Royal Canal. He died on 23 March, 1816, a year before its completion. He is buried alone in Kilbixy Graveyard near Ballynacarrigy. Buried alongside him marked with a much more elaborate tombstone is nine year old Alicia McMahon, eldest daughter of John McMahon, a partner in the firm of Henry, Mullins and McMahon. Alicia had died the previous year on 30 April 1815.

The only major problem encountered during the construction of the extension was malicious damage to the banks. This problem had been encountered initially in 1811 at Moyvalley where the canal had been opened eleven years earlier: breaches were made in the canal bank as a result of fears that the canal was going to be the cause of a local potato scarcity as large quantities of potatoes were being sent to the Dublin market by farmers with reasonable access to the canal. The cost of transporting potatoes was 1s-8d per ton from Mullingar to Dublin which was less than it cost farmers living within a five mile radius of the city to transport the same quantity.[49] Letters threatening to cut the banks and sink boats were received by the company and the boat owners and similar threats appear to have been received by the Grand Canal Company.

The reason the Royal Canal had such a good trade in the carriage of potatoes was the low rates charged, these rates having been set by the Directors of Inland Navigation in 1800. Potatoes were transported by the Royal Canal for ½d per ton per mile compared with 1½d per ton per mile by the Grand Canal. The offering of a reward for information and the threat of transportation for those caught causing damage helped to curtail the problem.

By 1814 during the construction of the western extension, the problem had returned. In July 1814[50] Henry, Mullins and McMahon, the contractors, reported to the Directors General "that a spirit of riot and combination had manifested itself to an alarming degree". On the night of 25 July for example, forty men armed with guns, swords and pistols had attacked the canal. Cars belonging to the

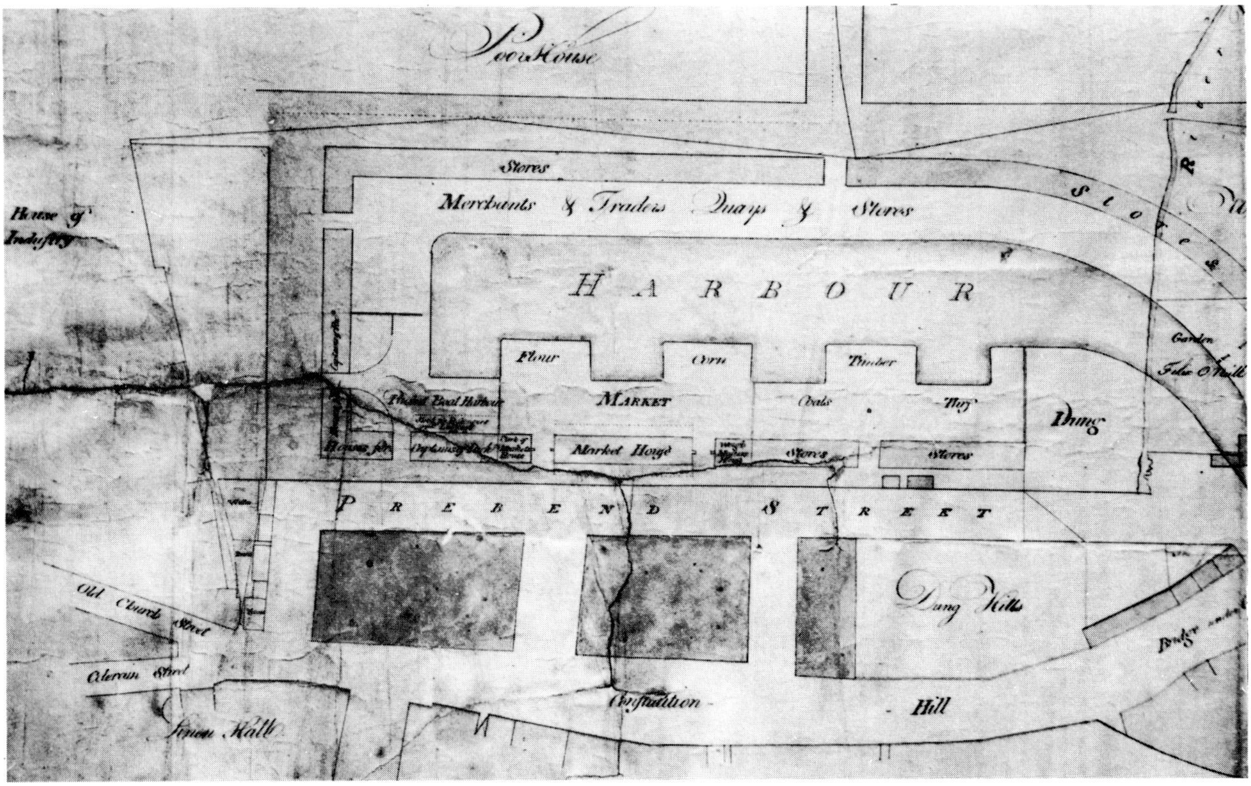

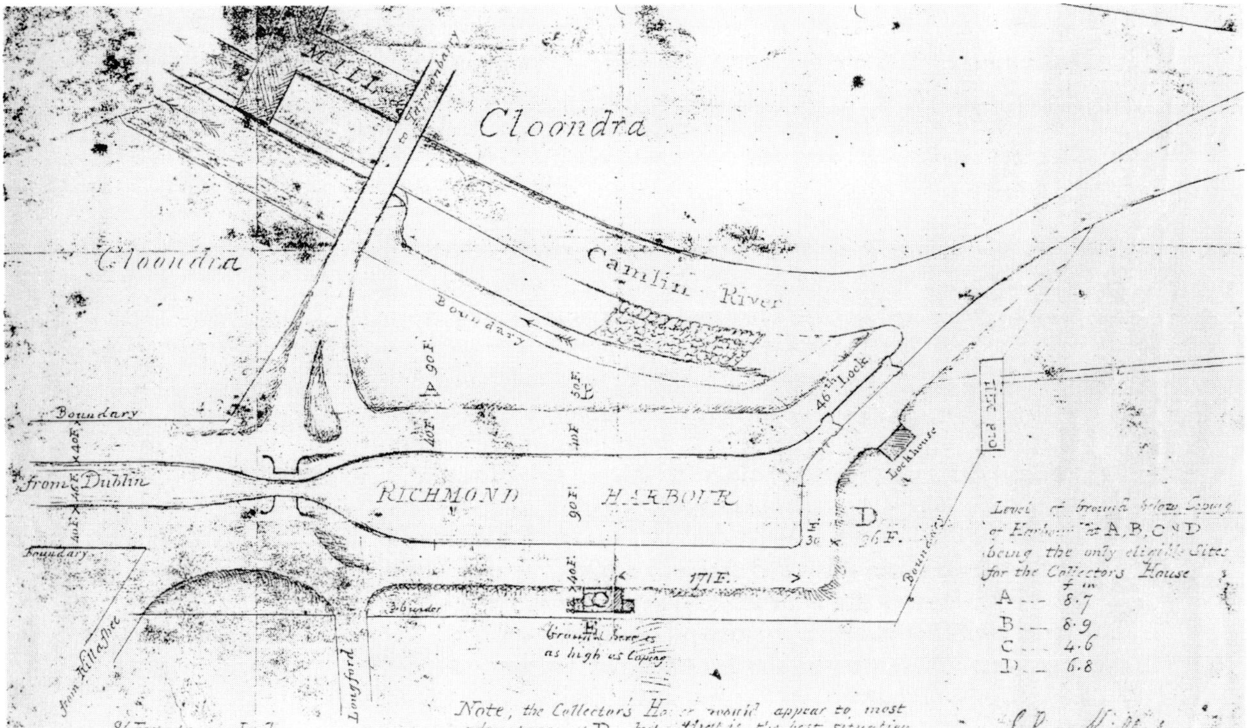

Figure 16: (top) Plan of Broadstone Harbour by Richard Evans, 1791. (City of Dublin Archive)
(bottom) Plan of Richmond Harbour by John Killaly, 1817.

company had been burnt and others broken into pieces.[51] Due to constant attacks, the contractors found it hard to continue the work and it became necessary for troops to be posted along the banks to protect the works and the labourers.[52] These attacks against the canal were instigated by the Ribbon Society.

These difficulties nothwithstanding, the extension from Coolnahay to Cloondara was completed with no major difficulties on the 26 May 1817 on time and at a cost of £145,000.

The main line of the canal including the branch to Broadstone Harbour took twenty-seven years to complete at a total cost of £1,421,954.[53] A total of forty-six locks plus a sea lock were built and thirty-nine harbours, twenty-eight of which were situated between Dublin and Mullingar and the remaining eleven between there and Cloondara.[54] The two largest and most important harbours to be constructed were Broadstone Harbour in Dublin and Richmond Harbour at Cloondara, county Longford. The docks which the company proposed to build at the Liffey in 1790 were abandoned and never completed although they appear on maps of the period. The complete project also included a number of canal-side stores and lock-keepers' houses. Although the number of houses built is not known, many still exist and some are still inhabited.

The Longford Branch

Pressure to extend the canal to Longford town was being exerted on the canal company from as early as 1822. In a letter[55] from the Longford town traders to the Royal Canal Company directors in August of that year the advantages of such an extension were highlighted. It was pointed out that the town had a large market and was a more prosperous location than the canal's existing termination point at the "Bleak harbour on the Shannon". Furthermore, the town could provide excellent accommodation for those passengers travelling on the boats.

In April 1823, a survey was carried out on a five mile line from Killashee on the main line to Longford town by J. J. Byrne, surveyor and William Tarrent, company engineer.[56] They estimated that the proposed branch line would cost £17,148-2-10 and, on this basis, funding was sought from the Exchequer Loan Commissioners, a body which the government had established in 1817 in an attempt to try to relieve distress and poverty. The commissioners were empowered to finance schemes which would provide employment and improve the country's economy. On 27 September 1823, agreement was reached whereby the funding would be provided on condition that the deeds for the entire line were lodged as collateral. While this arrangement was acceptable to the majority of the company directors, it was unacceptable to Bernard Mullins, a partner in the firm of Henry, Mullins and McMahon who had recently been elected as a director. Mullins was of the opinion that the estimate for the branch was too high and he believed it could be built for £10,500[57] and that only the tolls on the new branch should be mortgaged. This arrangement was unacceptable to the loan commissioners who offered £5,430 towards the work on the basis of mortgaging the tolls only. Rejection of this offer by the company forced it to undertake the building of the branch out of its own financial resources.

Tenders for the construction of the new branch were opened on 3 May 1827 and a contract was awarded on 31 July to John McMahon to build it for £8,750, completion to be by 10 November 1828. Controversy arose as to how the contract was awarded. Henry, Mullins and McMahon, the firm that had built the canal from Coolnahay to Cloondara had been dissolved in January 1827.[58] McMahon had remained in business while his two former partners, Henry and Mullins, were now on the board of directors that awarded the contract. Insinuations were made that McMahon had inside knowledge of the other tenders received, although this was never proved.

While there were no locks on the five mile branch to Longford, it was not as simple to construct as McMahon had anticipated: difficulties with rock at Newtown and near Garvagh slowed down progress. The harbour at Longford town was made larger than first planned. The branch was opened on 18 January 1830 at a final cost of £12,651.[59]

CHAPTER FOUR

Trade and Travel 1796-1845

The Opening of the Canal to Passenger Traffic

Prior to the arrival of the canals in Ireland, horse-drawn coaches and cars were the popular means of transporting people. It was not until the end of the eighteenth century that passenger travel began to flourish on the canals.[1] Apart from cheaper fares, many people preferred to travel by canal because it was more comfortable, less tiring and more reliable than road travel. The passengers were able to enjoy the scenery at a leisurely pace and had the added facility of being able to dine on board during the journey.

The Royal Canal Company commenced its passenger service on 2 December 1796,[2] between Dublin and Kilcock. Two boats, *The Camden* and *The Phelan*, operated with only one intermediate stop at Leixlip Aqueduct in each direction. One boat left Dublin at 9.00 a.m. each morning while the other left Kilcock simultaneously. The fare was 1s-1d first class cabin and 6d second class cabin from Dublin to Leixlip and the same from Leixlip to Kilcock. These fares were much lower than by coach or car travel. The cost of a journey from Dublin to Leixlip was 8s-8d by coach or 2s-3d by noddy car. The noddy was a low, covered vehicle with the shafts well up, which nodded as it moved. The driver sat so that the rump of the horse was at his mouth, and his rump was at the mouth of the person being carried, and "only the lowest order of citizens" used the noddy.[3] In 1799, the canal service was extended to Cloncurry, county Meath and later to Newcastle, near Enfield, with additional stops at Clonsilla, county Dublin and Maynooth and Ferns Lock, county Kildare.[4] The income from passenger boats between 1796 and 1800 amounted to £2,780-12s-7d.

Annual Passenger Revenue between 1796 and 1800 inclusive.

Year	Annual Revenue (Passengers and Goods)[5]	Passenger Revenue (including small parcels.)[6]	
	£	£	
1796	108- 1-11	37-6-6½	Dec. only.
1797	954- 8-11	946-7-0	
1798	711-16-1	567-3-1	
1799	996-11-3	729-1-4½	
1800	1583- 5-8	500-0-0	first four months.
Total	£4,355-7-10	£2,780-12-7	

The number of passengers who travelled is not known. It can be assumed that the majority of the passenger traffic was between Dublin and Leixlip, county Kildare. The scenery around the Salmon Leap on the river Liffey had established Leixlip as a tourist attraction in the middle of the eighteenth century and it was frequented by day visitors from Dublin.[7] The discovery of a spa by workmen digging the canal in 1791[8] dramatically increased the number of visitors to the village. It was estimated that on one Sunday in August 1794[9] between six o'clock in the morning and five o'clock in the evening fifty-five coaches, twenty-nine post-chaises, twenty-five noddy cars, eighty-two jaunting cars, twenty jigs, six open landaus, two hundred and twenty-one common cars, four hundred and fifty horsemen and numerous pedestrians entered Leixlip from the Dublin direction.

The canal passenger terminal in Leixlip was situated on the east side of the aqueduct and close to the spa. Because of the cheaper fare and the novelty of travelling by canal, many coach passengers must have transferred to the new transport system. Kilcock, the terminus for boats from 1796 until 1799, did not have the same attraction as Leixlip,

Figure 17: Leixlip Spa near the Rye Aqueduct.

and while some passengers probably travelled from Dublin to Kilcock and back, this was not possible in the same day because of the schedule. Thus these were more likely journeys of necessity rather than pleasure.

From the beginning of the operation, revenue from the passenger boats increased at a steady pace. The only exception to the steady rise in income occurred in 1798 when passenger revenue was £567-3-1, only half what it had been the previous year. Passenger traffic throughout the country was affected during this period by the rebellion, with coaches being attacked frequently.[10]

Canal traffic was also affected, persistent attacks on the Grand Canal forcing closure for a period.[11] While boats continued to ply the Royal Canal, it carried much reduced traffic.

Although total revenue for the years 1801 to 1806 is known, no breakdown of the percentage of income accounted for by the passenger trade is available. During this period, passenger fares more than doubled and more stopping places were introduced – at Moyvalley, Boyne Aqueduct, Thomastown and Mullingar. The increase in fares would have contributed to the rise in revenue. In addition, it is likely that the passenger trade continued to account for a large percentage of total revenue.

Total Annual Revenue from 1800-1806[12]

Year	Revenue
1801	£1,958- 2-0
1802	2,724- 1-8
1803	1,832- 1-0
1804	2,948-12-3
1805	3,306-19-8
1806	4,372-10-5

Expansion of the Service

As the canal extended westwards, the passenger service expanded. Every effort was made to encourage people to use the service, and coaches were provided to convey intending passengers from surrounding areas to points of embarkation on the canal. In 1806, for example, before the canal reached Mullingar, a coach service operated between the town and Thomastown Harbour for intending passengers to and from Dublin.[13] In addition to the boat fare of 10s-3½d, the coach cost 4s-4d to Mullingar and an extra 9s-9½d if the passenger wished to continue to Longford town.[14] When the canal reached Mullingar, a coach service was provided to Longford, Rooskey, Rathowen, Aughamore, Drumsna, Jamestown, Carrick-on-Shannon, Boyle and intermediate points.

The arrival of the canal at Mullingar in 1806 and the addition of two extra passenger boats in the following year increased the annual income of the canal company from £4,372-10-5 in 1806 to £9,989-13-2 in 1807. As in previous years, the number of passengers carried is unknown. The annual revenue from trade boats between 1807 and 1811 is known and by subtracting this from annual income it is possible to calculate revenue earned from the passenger traffic. Although these figures cannot be substantiated because, small parcels were carried in the passage boats, they indicate that substantial numbers of passengers were using the service during this period and that it was still expanding.

Total Revenue,[16] Revenue From Trade Boats[17] and Approximate Passenger Revenue from 1807-1811

Year	Total Revenue A	Revenue From Trade Boats B	Approximate Passenger Revenue A minus B
1807	£9,989-13-2	£3,406-6- 7	£6,583- 6-7
1808	13,021-16-5	4,202-3- 0	9,719-13-4
1809	12,599- 0-5	4,638-0- 3	8,396-17-4
1810	15,024-10-6	5,025-7-11	9,999- 2-6
1811	15,172- 0-0[18]	6,230-3- 6	8,841-16-5

Passenger numbers began to decline on Irish canals from about 1810. The novelty of travelling by canal which helped to establish the service had faded. Competition from road transport had also increased. In 1810, the Grand Canal Company was forced to reduce passenger fares because of this competition[19] and in the following year, four of their ten passenger boats were withdrawn from service.[20] A reduction of service from four boats to two on the Royal Canal in 1814 would suggest that similar problems were being encountered. By 1818, the yearly revenue on the Royal Canal had diminished considerably even though the canal itself had been considerably extended and a number of passenger stops added.

Stage Points and Passenger Fares From Dublin to Mullingar 1807[15]

Stage Points	Miles from Dublin	First Class s-d	Second Class s-d
Clonsilla	6	1-7½	1-1
Rye Aqueduct	9	2-6	1-7½
Maynooth	12	3-6	2-4
Kilcock	15	4-4	2-8½
Ferns Lock	16½	4-10½	3-0
Newcastle	21	6-6	3-9½
Moyvalley	24	7-7	4-4
Boyne Aqueduct	26	8-8	4-10½
Thomastown	33	10-3½	6-0
Mullingar	42	12-6	7-7

Passenger Traffic and the New Royal Canal Company

There are no year-by-year records of trade or revenue on the Royal Canal between 1811 and 1818. When the canal was completed to the Shannon in 1818, it was handed over in October to the new Royal Canal Company. As stated already, the new company inherited a passenger service which had declined considerably. The accounts for the half-year ending 31 March 1819[21] which was the first six months of operation under the new company, show a revenue from passenger service of £2,305-19-10 which is a considerable drop on the income of 1811.

Other parts of the service were losing money also. The stage between Ballymahon and Mullingar was operating at so great a loss that the company considered confining service to the profitable section of the line which was between Dublin and Mullingar.[22] Although this plan was not implemented, a re-organisation of the service took place. The two boats withdrawn in 1814 were reinstated. Boats now left Dublin and Mullingar at 6.00 p.m. the same evening. A new night service was introduced between Dublin and Killashee, county Longford, leaving Dublin at 2.00 p.m. every day and arriving at Killashee at 10.30 a.m. the following morning, returning from Killashee at 12.00 noon and arriving in Dublin at 9.30 a.m. the following day.

Competition from road transport forced a reduction in passenger fares but the costs incurred in operating the boats did not reduce proportionately: while the company owned the boats, the towing was contracted out to private individuals. A re-negotiation of the contract price from £50 per annum per mile to £46-13-4 per annum per mile in 1819 helped increase the company's income. In addition, extensive advertising and the re-establishment of connecting coaches from various towns in counties Westmeath, Sligo, Roscommon and Leitrim stimulated passenger traffic. The result was that for the six months to September 1819 the revenue increased to £4,330-14-11[23] compared with £2,305-19-10 for the previous six months.[24]

Stage Points and Passenger Fares from Dublin to Mullingar 1819[25]

Stages	Miles from Dublin	First Class	Second Class
		s-d	s-d
Clonsilla	6	1-3	0-10
Rye Aqueduct	9	1-11	1-3
Maynooth	12	2-6	1-8
Kilcock	15	3-2	2-1
Ferns Lock	17	3-6	2-11
Newcastle	21	4-4	2-11
Moyvalley	24	5-0	3-4
Boyne Aqueduct	26	5-5	3-8
Thomastown	33	6-10	4-2
Downs Bridge	37	7-8	4-7
Mullingar	41	8-6	5-0

Royal Canal Hotels

The company built two hotels to complement the passenger service: one at Broadstone Harbour in Dublin and another at Moyvalley, county Meath. A third hotel which was to be built in Mullingar never materialised, although plans and specifications for the buildings were drawn up. Very little is known about the hotel at Broadstone. The accounts relating to it are not mentioned in the Minute Book of the new Royal Canal Company. It is unlikely that it was a commercial success. It was last advertised as a hotel in *The Gentleman's and Citizens' Almanac* in 1812. The property was purchased in 1789 along with some land from a Mrs. Meredith for £1,500.[26] It was used originally as the company's offices and later converted to a hotel. As part of this property the company also acquired a small piece of land adjoining the Tolka river at Glasnevin village. It was purchased from them in 1818 by the Royal Dublin Society and is now the Rose Garden of the National Botanic Gardens.

Figure 18: Part of the old Royal Canal Hotel at Broadstone as it exists today.

Unlike the hotel at Broadstone, the hotel at Moyvalley was purpose built and opened on 20 October 1807.[27] Prices ranged from 1s-1d for a bed for a servant to 4s-4d for one of the four best bed chambers. No account of earnings are available until 1819: in the half year ending March 1819[28] the revenue earned by the hotel was £7-1s-4d, while in the same year the salary paid to the hotel keeper was £100.[29] Whatever the initial success of the hotel, and it was probably limited, the drop in the number of passengers travelling on the canal between 1811 and 1818 must have caused a reduction in the number of people using the hotel. The location of the hotel, thirty-two miles from Dublin and twenty-one miles from Mullingar where overnight accommodation was plentiful for those travelling further also contributed to its failure. In addition, the schedules on the canal did not encourage a passenger to break a journey at Moyvalley and spend between 1s-1d and 4s-4d on accommodation: westbound passengers had to rise at 5.00 a.m. to catch a boat onwards while the east-bound morning boat left at 4.00 a.m.

As part of the re-organisation of the company, it was decided to set the hotel as a going concern. In October

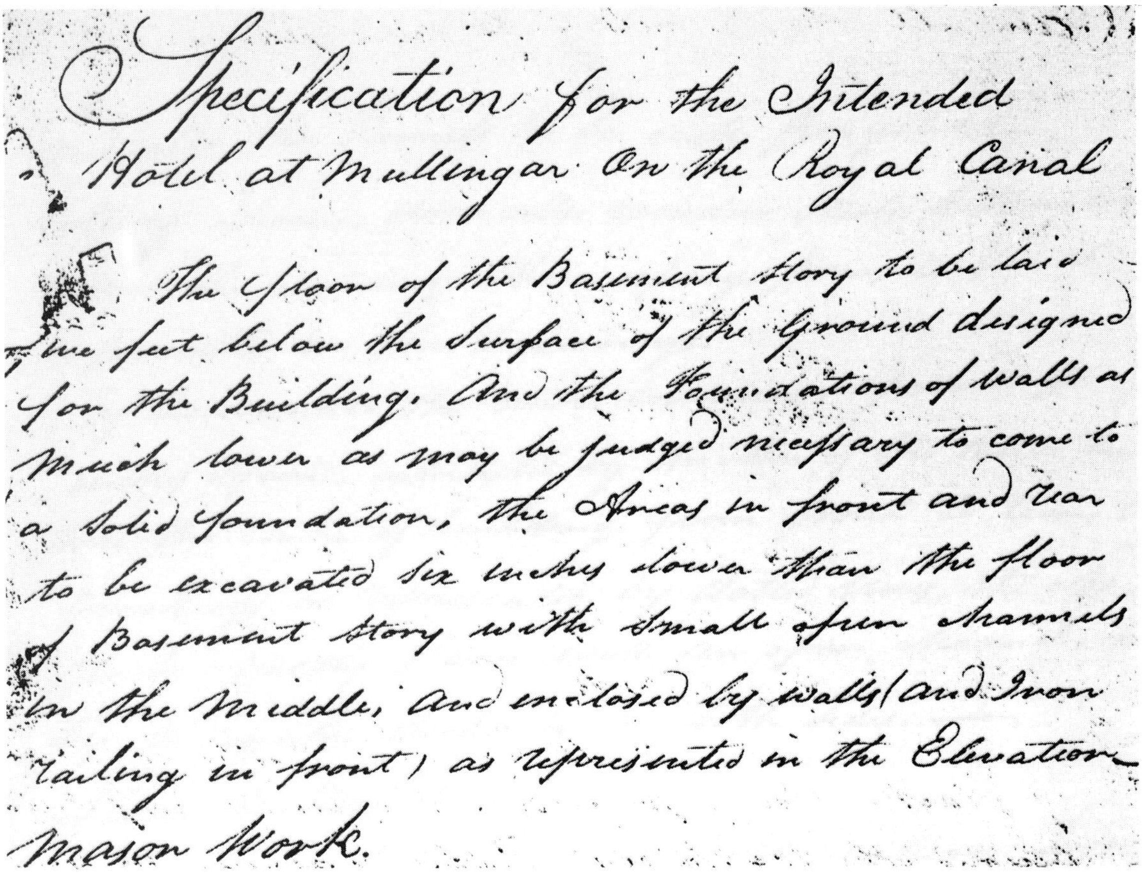

Specification for the Intended
Hotel at Mullingar On the Royal Canal

The Floor of the Basement Story to be laid five feet below the Surface of the Ground designed for the Building. And the Foundations of Walls as much lower as may be judged necessary to come to a Solid Foundation, the Areas in front and rear to be excavated six inches lower than the floor of Basement Story with small open channels in the Middle, and enclosed by walls (and Iron railing in front) as represented in the Elevation

Mason Work.

Figure 19: Extract from the specification for the Royal Canal Hotel at Mullingar which was never built.

1819, John Conroy rented it on a ninety-nine year lease at fifty guineas per annum.[30] However he was unsuccessful in his efforts to run it as a hotel and surrendered the lease on 16 April 1821[31] The building was not occupied again until October 1825 when a new tenant was found. Mark Flower agreed to take a ninety-nine year lease at sixty guineas a year with a view to setting up a pin factory[32] but he took the precaution of inserting a three year surrender clause. In 1828 Flower surrendered the lease and it was then leased to William Glynn at the same rent to be used as a corn depot and posting station on condition that his coaches must not interfere with the trade of the passenger boats. Glynn's efforts to run it as a general country store and coaching house were also unsuccessful and in an effort to keep him at Moyvalley as a tenant, the company reduced his rent to £30 per year in 1831. However his business continued to decline and in April 1832[33] he surrendered his lease because of "the almost total want of business". In 1833 John McCann, one of the canal traders, leased the premises and converted part of it to a corn store.

In 1848 the building was sold to John Switzer who established a hydropathic centre for people suffering from disease and chronic pain.[34] The centre was fitted out with a variety of hot and cold baths in which patients attending the centre were immersed. How long Mr. Switzer continued to run the centre is not known, but the family continued to live there until 1912 when it was sold to a Mr. Ross. In 1922 Mr. Ross sold the house to Dr. Carey who in turn sold it in 1929 to a local man Mr. Mulvanney. In 1930 Mr. Mulvanney moved from the house to a smaller one close by. The old house became derelict and fell into ruin. In 1974, the building was demolished in preparation for a new road and bridge.

The Introduction of the Fly Boats

The improvement in the roads and the inauguration of competing services by various road carriers continued in the 1820s to draw passengers from the canal. The canal company was forced on occasions to shelve its intention to raise fares because of competition from the road carriers.[35] The Mullingar to Dublin section of the canal carried the most passsenger traffic and therefore was most prone to competition. By 1823, the day boat had lost substantial numbers of passengers to the road carriers and to a night boat which had been introduced in 1819 between Dublin and Killashee and which proved very attractive to the travelling public. By 1822, the day boat was earning less than the £1,860 it cost annually to run the service. It was reduced to run three days a week in March 1824 leaving Dublin for Mullingar on Tuesday, Thursday and Saturday, returning on the following days. This increased the transfer of business from the day boat to the night boat which still ran seven nights per week and travelled beyond Mullingar. By 1825, only eighty-eight people travelled first class on the day boat between Dublin and Coolnahay in county Westmeath in the first six months of the year[36] while three hundred and forty-one travelled second class.

Passenger Boat Revenue from Dublin to Mullingar
for years ending 30 September 1819-1823.[37]

1819	£3,727-11- 0
1820	2,150- 5-11
1821	1,936-10- 1
1822	1,810-12-11
1823	1,383- 1- 3

By the 1830s, various towns in counties Westmeath, Longford, Roscommon, Leitrim and Sligo were still important centres for providing passenger traffic on the canal and the provision of private connecting coach services continued to be an integral part of the passenger service. Of the several carriers, the most noted was Charles Bianconi who, unlike the other carriers, was approached by the company in 1831 to provide a service. This he did, operating two horse cars from Athlone, county Westmeath to Toombridge and from Roscommon, Castlerea and Sligo to Longford town.[38]

Although six new passenger boats were built and put into service between 1826 and 1834[39] the passenger traffic continued to decline. The recruitment of Bianconi, who was the largest coach operator and had the reputation of being the most efficient carrier in the country, was an attempt to salvage the situation. With an efficient service like Bianconi's it was expected that passenger numbers would increase.

The continued competition from road carriers in the early 1830s, including Bianconi himself, forced the company to improve its service and to increase the speed of the boats. Thomas O'Neill, the company's boat inspector and dock master investigated[40] "Scotch Boats" also known as "Fly boats" which were in use on the Paisley Canal in Glasgow. These boats were capable of carrying one hundred and ten passengers at a speed of ten miles per hour. They were seventy feet long by five feet six inches wide and were made from sixteen gauge lightweight iron on timber ribs.[41] Several attempts by the Royal Canal Company to imitate these boats by reducing the weight and size of their existing passenger vessels had failed. It was thus decided that fly boats should be introduced on the canal and these went into service on 30 July 1833,[42] reducing the time of the journey from Dublin to Mullingar from twelve to eight hours. The boats were towed by two horses who galloped each stage of eight miles at twelve miles per hour. The fly boats operated between Dublin and Longford by day while the night boat became exclusively used by the poorer classes[43] at 1d per mile, a halfpenny less than the cost of the fly boat.

The introduction of the fly boats improved the service and helped to increase the number of passengers[44]. Although passenger traffic on the canal continued to grow in the concluding years of the 1830s and into the 1840s because of the introduction of the fly boats, the profit from the service was small. Parts of the canal were unsuitable for fly boats. The banks of sections such as at Cappagh Bog, county Kildare, the area through Cloncurry, county Meath and at Toomebridge, county Westmeath, were easily damaged by the wash from the boats and the towpaths were not strong enough to cope with galloping horses. Thus seven-eighths of the revenue earned from the fly boat service had to be used to repair the banks and the boats and to employ extra lock keepers. In the 1820s, a serious problem of water shortage due to locking up and down boats arose on the canal and hindered not only the passenger boats but also the trade boats. The shortage came about when industry which had located on the canal began to use the water supply. The introduction of the fly boats exacerbated the water supply situation particularly during the summer months and at times the canal was unable to operate.

It is not until the second report of the Railway Commissioners in 1838 that the numbers of passengers travelling on the canal become available. Between May 1836 and May 1837, 46,450 passengers were carried, 28,320 travelling by the night boat and 18,130 on the fly boat.

Passenger Traffic and the coming of the Railway

In 1844 the Board of the company received an offer for the purchase of the canal from the newly formed Midland Great Western Railway Company which was about to construct a parallel railway route. The canal company directors advised the shareholders to accept the offer and the entire line was sold for £318,860.[45] Although the Royal Canal Company received £298,059 the difference of £20,801 was invested as capital in the canal by the Railway Company. Between 28 June 1847 and 30 June 1848 17,740 first class passengers, 72,390 second class passengers and 170,494 third class passengers travelled on the Midland Great Western Railway between Dublin and Enfield in county Meath. By the time the railway reached Mullingar on 2 October 1848, 28,027 first class, 145,605 second class and 251,685 third class passengers had used the railway.[46] The canal service was unable to compete with rail travel and, not suprisingly, the railway company phased out the passenger boat service on the canal. In 1847 the fly boat was operating between Dublin and Mullingar only while the night boat was operating between Dublin and Longford.[47]

As the railway progressed westwards from Dublin it was built alongside the canal and service on the latter was further curtailed. During 1848 for example before the railway reached Mullingar, the passenger boats from Dublin were discontinued and boats only plied from Kinnegad station (Hill of Down) after meeting the 7.00 a.m. train from Dublin.[48] After the railway reached Mullingar at the end of 1848 the passenger boat service was discontinued and passengers who travelled to Mullingar by train were then carried further west by Bianconi coach and car.

The Midland Great Western Railway bought the Royal Canal with the intention of building the railway line in its bed, but were prevented from doing so. The railway company was not interested in the passenger traffic but rather in the acquisition of the canal property which provided them with an uninterrupted linear route from west of Dublin to Mullingar. The purchasing of such a property also avoided delays in acquiring land from landowners, allowing the work of building the railway line to commence immediately. Although it was not the prime motive for the purchase, the canal aided the building of the railway by providing a readymade transport system upon which to carry heavy goods and equipment needed in the construction.

The Beginning of Trade Boats on the Canal

No town or village along the route of the Royal Canal owes its origin to the development of the waterway. However many did expand and prosper in the late eighteenth and early nineteenth century due to its arrival. In effect, the canal transformed formerly landlocked towns and villages into inland ports, creating harbours and warehouses in places where none had existed. The growth of a town depended on the expansion of its trade[49] and trade could not expand unless transport facilities improved. The Irish road system, while adequate for the carrying of passengers and light goods, was unsuitable for the long-distance haulage of bulk goods[50] and rates were uncompetitive. Arthur Young in 1779[51] had high praise for Irish roads, but he was critical of the transport methods used. Carts were drawn by one horse only and those carts belonging to the poor were cheaply constructed and unfit for robust work. Young estimated that when hired by the day, the cost of a cart could be as much as five hundred per cent dearer than in England, due to the very small quantities carried and the slow pace of travel. Although the carts which worked regularly drawing flour from mills into Dublin were better constructed and carried loads of between six and ten hundredweight, Thomson[52] in 1802 estimated that the cost of road transport in county Meath was 9d per cwt. per ten miles (18d per ton per mile). Rates on the Royal Canal in 1801[53] ranged from 2d per ton per mile for general merchandise to ½d per ton per mile for potatoes. The arrival of the canal thus reduced transport costs dramatically. Bulk goods such as grain which were previously carried by road[54] were now transported by canal at a more economical rate. The benefit to market towns was enormous: accessibility to Dublin meant that the market economy could function fully. Prices were no longer fixed to a low local base but to those prevailing in Dublin.[55]

The first trade boats began to ply the Royal Canal between Dublin and Kilcock in May 1796.[56] These boats took longer to become established than the passenger boats. One of the principal causes of this in the early years was the unfinished state of the canal with only a short length in operation: it passed through only two villages, Maynooth and Kilcock in county Kildare. Existing trade by road between these centres and Dublin was well established and because of their relative proximity to the city, goods such as flour continued to be transported by road even after the arrival of the canal.[57] The lack of proper harbours influenced the situation also: while Kilcock had a harbour, Maynooth had none.[58] In Dublin, work on the docks at the North Wall had been abandoned while the Broadstone Harbour was still only under construction. Transport facilities to and from the canal itself were both poor and expensive and because of this farmers were reluctant to use the service.

Revenue from Tolls 1796-1800[59]

1796	£78-13- 9.	(May-December only)
1797	206- 4- 8	
1798	262-19-11	
1799	483- 5- 1	
1800	230- 5- 1	(First four months only)

The reduction in tolls imposed by the Directors General of Inland Navigation as part of their agreement to make funds available to the company to enable them to carry on with the work in 1801 seriously affected the earnings of the company from trade boats. This was the beginning of a boom period for Ireland. Exports rose by forty per cent between 1792 and 1815,[60] principally due to the war with France and the increased inability of England to supply its own food requirements. While the quantities of goods carried on the canal rose as work on extending it progressed, the revenue remained low. Tolls were received from by-traders who operated boats on the canal at the following rates[61]: 1d per mile per ton on corn, meal, malt, flour, potatoes, lime, sand, fuel or manure brought from Dublin and 2d per mile per ton on the same goods brought to Dublin.

Expansion and Arrival of the Canal in Mullingar

The arrival of the canal in Mullingar in December 1806 made a significant difference to the fortunes of the company. The income of £4,372-10-5d, at the end of 1806, had more than doubled to £9,989-13-2 by the end of 1807. Quantities of most goods being carried doubled during this period. By December 1808, when John Brownrigg made a second report[62] for the Directors General of Inland Navigation, Broadstone Harbour was in operation: two wharves were in use and a third marked out awaiting construction. Some stores were also built, but how many, or who occupied them, is not stated. Mullingar had two harbours, one for passengers and a second for trade, and some stores and graving docks were also in operation. Between 1807 and 1811 approximately seventeen different types of goods were being carried on the canal on a regular basis. These goods can be broadly broken into three main types: general merchandise, building materials and agricultural produce. Although an increase is recorded in the quantity of most goods carried, building materials account for the largest increase. While the type and quantities of the goods carried is known their distribution along the canal is not and therefore it is not possible to give the locations to which goods such as building materials were brought. However as the carrying of those items peaked at the time when Broadstone Harbour was still under construction it is most likely that the majority of building materials were carried to Dublin.

Limestone increased from 2,629 tons in 1807 to 11,072 tons in 1808 and sand and gravel increased from 1,212 tons in 1807 to 3,258 tons in 1811, much of this being probably used to build the walls of the wharves at Broadstone described by John Brownrigg in 1808. Stone flags which increased from 8,689 tons in 1808 to 13,102 tons in 1809 were probably used to pave the floor of the new harbour. Similarly the tonnage of bricks carried increased from 5,108 tons in 1810 to 11,622 in 1811 and much of this increase was most likely used for the building of stores at Broadstone and at other harbours along the route.

A drop is recorded in quantities of some types of goods being carried. Malt, for instance, dropped from 129 tons in 1807 to only 3 tons in 1811. The decrease in the quantity of malt and the increase in grain from 2,954 tons in 1807 to 9,236 tons in 1811 are linked. Large quantities of Irish grain were exported during this period but the Irish distilleries also began to use considerable quantities. Prior to 1800, the use of raw grain alone was prohibited in distilling whiskey in Ireland and distillers used a mixture of malt and some raw grain.[63] In 1800, this changed and distillers were free to use only as much malt as was needed to generate fermentation in the raw grain. As duty was paid on malt, the distilling industry changed quickly to using grain spirit which became the characteristic of Irish whiskey of the nineteenth century. Thus the quantities of malt being carried on the canal for use in the distilling industry decreased while the carrying of grain increased.

Between 1796 and 1800[64] twenty-two tons of goods were carried along the canal. Between 1807 and 1811 when the canal had reached Coolnahay, sixty miles from Dublin, the tonnage reached 252,203 tons 30 cwts.

There is no record of the activity and revenue of the company between 1811 and 1818. An examination of the Dublin Street Plans attached to the *Dublin Directory* of 1815 and 1816 shows that a re-organisation of the stores at Broadstone took place at some time in this period. The 1816 map shows new stores closer to the water's edge while much of the building shown on the 1815 map has been demolished. It may be assumed that the new buildings were built of brick or stone and that they replaced existing timber structures or badly positioned brick ones.

The completion of the canal to the Shannon was the primary objective of the Directors General of Inland Navigation and, during their period of control, the condition of many of the stores on those parts of the canal already completed appears to have deteriorated. Thus, the commissioners often offered prospective new tenants the option of reduced rents, and, in many cases, exemptions from rent for the first year in return for repairing the buildings.

By 1 October 1818 when the new directors had taken over the running of the company, six stores were in existence at Broadstone and six at Mullingar,[65] all occupied by traders operating boats on the canal. The new directors raised the rents of these stores by £5 per annum, all rents to be paid six months in advance. Notices of rent increase were sent to the following traders at Mullingar: Alexander Boggie Store 2, Nooney and Carroll Stores 3 and 4. F. & J. Pillsworth 5 and 6, and Carroll and Bathurst Store 1. The tolls which had been fixed in 1801 were increased by 1½d per mile and 1d extra per lock.[66] These measures combined with a more positive approach resulted within a short period in increased revenue.

Receipts and Expenditure for Years Ending, September 1817, 1818, 1819, 1820 and 1821

	Receipts for years ending 30 September.	Expenditure for years ending 30 September.
1817	10,676-15-10	24,124-19-5
1818	15,441-14-11	25,771-19-8
1819	21,312-11- 1*	12,793-16-2
1820	20,002- 6- 1	18,599-16-4
1821	33,141- 0- 5	15,759-12-1

* First six months under management of new directors.

The completion of the canal and more positive management also stimulated a new attitude among the existing traders. Several began to expand their businesses by acquiring plots of ground and erecting new stores. Competition between traders for the existing unoccupied stores at Broadstone and Mullingar was keen with several bids often being received for the same store. Bids from F. J. Pillsworth and John Fay of £10 each for a store at Broadstone were rejected, the lease being granted to Samuel Manning who bid £15 p.a. for the store.[67] Business was brisk and trade on the canal had begun to flourish by 1819. There was no shortage of enquiries as to when the company would make available plots for store building at the various harbours along the route.

The demand for imported goods, such as timber, slate and particularly English coal, was brisk in the small villages along the route at this time. Indeed, such was the demand that the space provided by the company at the various harbours now became inadequate. A fire at the harbour in Mullingar on Friday 14 December 1821[68] destroyed the stores of F. & J. Pillsworth, the largest trader on the canal, but it did not interrupt or damage the firm's business. Seizing upon the opportunity to expand, they obtained leases on Stores 3 and 4 (they already occupied Store 5) and rented back their burnt out Store 6 to use as a yard from which to sell and distribute coal.

Mullingar was the largest town on the route and it was to be expected that canal trade to and from the town would be busy. However, other small villages also began to experience a growth and traders who had set up in such places as Richmond Harbour in the village of Cloondara, county Longford, the termination point of the canal, were soon seeking additional space as their businesses were expanding rapidly.

Two types of trader existed at Cloondara. The first were bye traders who acted as carriers and who stored goods in rented accommodation at the harbour. The second type were traders who rented plots of ground and built a store from which they distributed and sold goods to the surrounding hinterland. One such trader was Valentine Skipton who in 1821[69] was granted a lease to build two stores, each thirty feet by twenty feet. By 1822, his business had expanded so much that he was seeking additional ground in order to store slate, timber, coal and other bulky goods.[70] Cloondara village had no market and although the harbour had direct access to the Shannon, the success of the town appears to have been localised. Certainly, the small village of Cloondara was unable to sustain its position once the canal branch to Longford was completed.

After 1811 no details of freight carryings are available until 1836. By 1836, the principal commodities being carried were corn, flour, potatoes, pigs, cattle, turf, imported coal and general merchandise. Although the quantities of some items fluctuated according to the seasons, harvests and economic conditions in the country, the total tonnage carried increased at a slow but steady pace. An increase in agricultural exports such as grain (which increased from 1,000,000 quarters at the beginning of the century to 3,000,000 quarters per annum in 1837-38[71]) and livestock such as pigs is reflected in the data.

Because of the canal's dependence on agricultural produce, adverse conditions such as a poor harvest as occurred in 1833 and 1838 affected the quantities of goods carried. In 1836, for example, the quantity of corn-meal, potatoes, butter and pigs carried was 75,387 tons as compared to 23,725 tons 9 cwts. in 1839 after a bad harvest.

Development of Canal-Side Industries

Warehousing and facilities for the distribution of goods followed the canal as a related canal-side industry. In addition, some small local enterprises emerged chiefly connected with harvesting, turf processing and the manufacture of bricks. Only in the greater Dublin area did any large-scale canal-side manufacturing industry develop.

Between 1821 and 1830, leases for a number of mill sites were granted between Drumcondra Road and

Blanchardstown. The establishment of these mills was as a result of an existing mill[72] at the first lock (North Wall) being supplied with canal water which prompted a demand in the 1820s for canal-side industrial sites which would be similarly supplied. Within a short period, four leases were granted. Only one of the mills created was established as a corn mill; the other three were used for different purposes. In 1822, a lease was granted to John Hills[73] for a "mill" site between Drumcondra Road and Glasnevin Road to be used to manufacture glass. A similar lease was granted[74] to John Mallett at the 5th lock where an iron mill was established. Finally, a woollen mill was established by Thomas Bryan at the 12th lock in Blanchardstown.[75] The corn mill was established at the 6th lock by Thomas Duffy. Duffy, whose brother was an existing bye trader on the canal, also established stores at Broadstone and Mullingar harbours.

Figure 20: Mallett's Mill at the 5th lock (Cross Guns Bridge) now being developed as apartments.

The prime factor in causing the establishment of the foregoing industries at the canal side was the apparent availability of water. However, it emerged later that the canal was unable to supply a sufficient amount of water to operate the mills,[76] with water being especially scarce for four months of the year. Apart from having to maintain a constant supply for the boats and the industries, the company was also supplying water to Dublin Corporation for the north city reservoir.[77] Thus although several enquiries were received, no further expansion of canal-side mill industries took place beyond Blanchardstown. In 1825, requests to supply water to proposed breweries at Broadstone in Dublin[78] and at Ballynacarrigy in county Westmeath were rejected[79] presumably because of the water supply situation. An application for a site at the 17th lock by Mr. Greenham to set up a cotton mill which would employ three to five hundred people also appears to have been refused[80] probably for the same reason. It must, therefore, be assumed that the lack of a sufficient supply of water was the main disincentive to further developments of canal-side industries on the eastern stretch of the canal.

The Turf Industry and the Canal

Smaller less structured industries, chiefly connected with turf, emerged along the canal. Small plots of bog were rented to induviduals to harvest and to save turf. A large turf market developed at Mullingar[81] and a smaller one at Cope Bridge[82] near Leixlip in county Kildare. Yards selling and distributing turf were also developed in Dublin. The largest at Broadstone was run by the Irish Turf Company while a smaller one was established at Whitworth Road, Glasnevin between Westmoreland Bridge and Binns Bridge. Turf was sold also from boats, and traders from as far as county Longford had no difficulty in disposing of boatloads of turf between the 13th lock and Dublin city.[83]

The movement of bulky goods such as turf was slow and expensive by road. The canal changed this situation and made turf freely available in large quantities at the Dublin market at competitive prices. The market for turf was already well established in the city with the turf coming mainly from the nearest large bog, the Bog of

Allen. Turf-cutting had begun on a large scale at the end of the eighteenth century to supply the Dublin market[84] and more than 300,000 tons from the Bog of Allen was being sold annually in the city during the first half of the nineteenth century. The advent of the Royal Canal opened up this market to the areas along its route where bogland existed. For those living along the canal, the market for their turf changed from one supplying local needs only to one supplying the Dublin market where profits were greater.

The area which derived most benefit from the sale of turf was that around Kilcock and the Bog of Cappagh in county Kildare. Between 1 May 1821 and 28 January 1822 forty-three boat loads were sent to Dublin[85] at an average of ninety tons per load. The canal company encouraged the turf industry in its area and granted leases on plots of bog to those who would cut and sell the turf. One such lease was granted to Martin Connaughton for a plot at the Bog of Cappagh for seven years at a rent of £50 per annum. Connaughton estimated that he could cut and sell eighty boat loads per year at the Dublin market.[86]

Transporting turf provided the Royal Canal Company with a major source of revenue. The quantities carried rose from 3,585 tons in 1811 to a maximum of 82,988 tons in 1839. In 1822, the road competitors threatened the dominant position of the canal as the main transporter of turf by reducing their rates and by 1824, the supply of turf by canal to the market at Mullingar was experiencing extreme difficulties with the road carriers selling it at 6d per ton cheaper.[87] To rectify this position the canal company was forced to reduce its tolls on turf and, to further encourage the industry, turf banks were given free to those who would cut turf and transport it by canal.[88]

Because the canal passed through the middle of the Bog of Cappagh, turf-cutting developed in the area on a large scale. The presence of a transport system passing through the bog to carry away the turf also influenced the siting of the first factory in Ireland to process turf mechanically. In 1844[89] Charles Wye Williams, a businessman and inventor, built a factory on the south bank of the canal at the Bog of Cappagh whereby wet turf fibres were squeezed dry and moulded into dry turf sods. The freshly dried peat was then broken up into fibre strands, enveloped in cloths, placed in a powerful press and pressurised until it was reduced to one third of its original volume and three-fifths of its original weight. After this process the turf was allowed to dry in the open air and sold ex works at 5s per ton. Although most probably a superior fuel to sod turf, the price was too great relative to that for hand-cut turf which sold ex works at 3s-6d per ton. As a result, the factory closed in 1849.

Although the foregoing operation failed at Cappagh, it had two important consequences for the Irish peat industry. Through his business connections, Williams introduced turf as a fuel to the Inland Navigation Company who used it on their Shannon boats. This was among its first industrial utilizations. Williams also pioneered the manufacture of peat charcoal in Ireland.

Attacks on the Canal and Disruption to Trade

Attacks on the canal which were prevalent in 1814-15 and to which reference has been made already began again in 1820. Potato failure in 1817 and 1819 brought much suffering to the poor. Famine had become widespread by 1822[90] and chronic unemployment was a feature of the economy. A scarcity of food and, more important, a need to create employment by the perpetrators of the damage was the prime motive in the malicious attacks. The first of these occurred in February 1820 at the Blackwater aqueduct[91] in county Kildare. As a result of the breach created, major disruption was caused to the business of the canal. The fact that over one hundred local men turned up ready to work the following morning gives some indication of the scale of the damage and of the unemployment situation in the area. A wage of 5s per week was demanded which forced the company to employ labourers from Dublin and Mullingar who would work for a lower rate. This resulted in further outbreaks of violence where workers were threatened and stoned. Although the Moyvalley area was where the majority of the incidents occurred, similar attacks became widespread throughout the entire length of the canal, with instances being reported at Mullingar and Longford.

Attacks on the canal banks and on the trade and passenger boats was a feature of life on the canal throughout the 1820s. It was common for boats to be attacked, the driver and crew to be beaten up and the boat to be sunk.[92] Constant pressure from the boat owners and traders for protection forced the company to provide military escorts for the passage through the villages and towns along the route. As a result of the attacks, trade was affected severely. Several traders threatened to withdraw their boats altogether as they began to regard the canal "as not a reliable mode of conveyance".[93]

Further disruption to trade on the canal came from drivers employed by the boat owners and traders. In June 1822, one of the contractors engaged to provide horses to pull the passage boats complained that "Latterly the ribbon system got to such a head, he had no power or control whatever on his drivers".[94] The Ribbon Society or more commonly known as Ribbonmen, was an illegal, secret organisation which operated mainly in the south and west of Ireland, but was known to have members in Meath and Westmeath.[95] The membership of the organisation was entirely Roman Catholic and from the poorer classes. While their aim was to recover land confiscated from Catholics, they used any means to upset the government and establishment, and in particular such bodies as the police. The disruption of trade on the canal was used by the Ribbon Society to intimidate the canal directors and shareholders, many of whom were landlords. Traders had no choice but to agree to higher wages to be paid in advance.[96] Those who worked for reduced wages were beaten up.

The outbreaks of violence led on occasion to the closure of the canal[97] and the suspension of trade for periods of up to a month. This affected the revenue of the canal company and also contributed to a general loss of trade. At the same time, the company was under constant pressure to reduce tolls, especially by 1830 when serious competition had emerged from the road carriers.

The completion of the western stretch of the canal from Coolnahay to the Shannon failed to bring the expected boost in carryings from the north. The opening of the Lough Allen Canal in 1820 which linked Battlebridge on the river Shannon to Lough Allen near Arigna was a further disappointment as the expected trade in coal from Arigna failed to materialise. The principal cause of these problems was the defective shallow state of the upper Shannon which was unsuitable for deeper draft steamers, which could not go north of Athlone.[98] The smaller boats passing between Carrick-on-Shannon and Rooskey were forced to unload part of their cargo if it exceeded 25 tons. In September 1821, a request from the Royal Canal Company for 1,000 tons of coal could not be delivered because of this problem. While it was possible to transport small loads the cost was uneconomic. The overall effect of this situation on the Royal Canal was effectively to confine its commercial traffic to the towns and villages on its route and to a narrow hinterland on each side. Little benefit ever accrued from the river Shannon connection.

Chapter Five

The Royal Canal and the Railway

As previously stated, the primary objective of the Midland Great Western Railway Company in acquiring the Royal Canal in 1845 was to build the railway line in the bed of the canal.[1] This suggestion was put forward in 1845 by the Duke of Leinster, son of the original canal director, who stated in a letter on behalf of the railway company to the Board of Control[2] that to abandon the canal would be more beneficial to the public. His idea was not shared by the Board of Control or by the shareholders of the Royal Canal Company and it is most probably due to this opposition that in Acts 8 and 9 Victoria c.119 which allowed the railway company to acquire the canal, a condition was laid down that the canal must remain a separate transport system.

Although the canal was owned by the railway company after 1845, Section 36 of the aforementioned Act continued to allow considerable control over the affairs of the canal to be exercised by the Lord Lieutenant and the Board of Control. The railway company had to "maintain, uphold and preserve all the works for the purpose of navigation in as full, ample and perfect a manner as required by the Act of 1818". They could not increase rents or tolls without the consent of the Lord Lieutenant and the Board of Control. A further Act passed in 1846[3] deemed the Midland Great Western Railway Company and the Royal Canal Company as one company and confirmed these powers. In effect the only benefit acquired by the Midland Great Western Railway Company in purchasing the canal (apart from the income collected from tolls and rents from stores) was the acquisition of one hundred and ninety-four acres of Royal Canal Company land upon which the railway line was

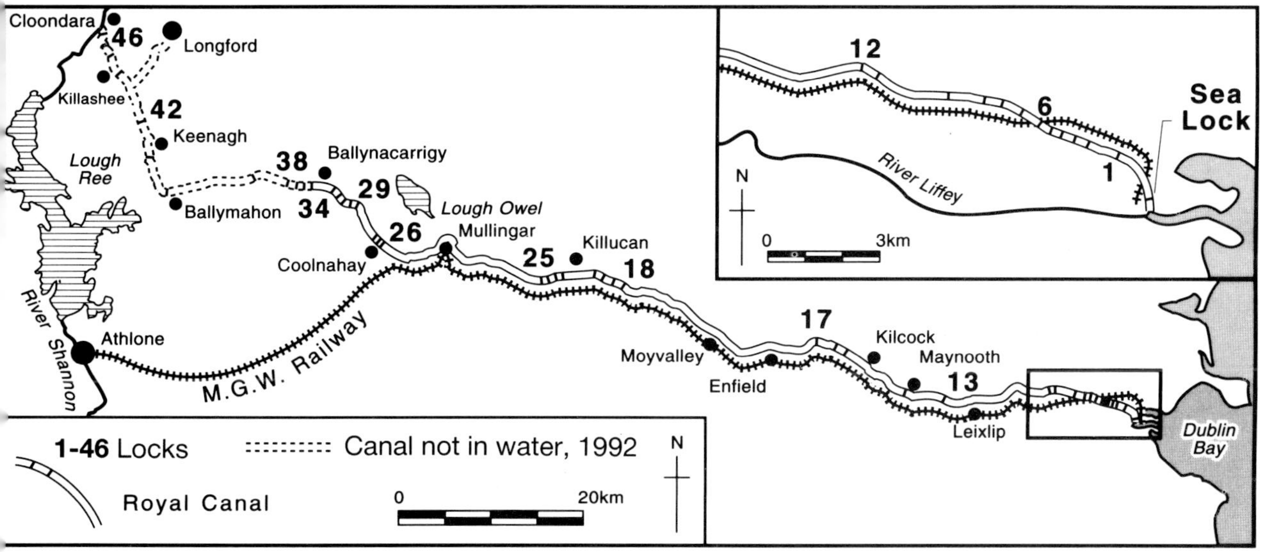

Figure 21: Map showing the Midland Great Western Railway line alongside the Royal Canal and the position of the forty seven locks.

built: twenty-four acres within the Dublin city boundary and one hundred and seventy acres outside.[4]

The railway was constructed alongside the canal from Dublin to approximately four miles beyond Mullingar. On this section seventeen railway stations were built in towns and villages where canal wharfs existed. The remaining eleven wharfs on the canal were situated in the Dublin area and in countryside remote from towns and villages of significant size. West of Mullingar the railway was constructed away from the canal, rejoining it at Longford town.

Table of Canal Towns and Villages West of Mullingar not served directly by Railway.[5]

Name of Village	Distance from Railway Station
Ballynacarrigy	7 miles
Abbeyshrule	8 miles
Ballymahon	10 miles
Keenagh	6 miles
Killashee	4 miles
Cloondara	6 Miles

The Transfer from Canal to Railway

The transfer of goods carried by canal to rail transport was not immediately noticeable. A reduction of twenty-five per cent on tolls was introduced in 1845. This reduction was negotiated by the canal company on behalf of the canal traders when the railway company took possession of the canal.[6] During the early years of the period 1846-1851 the tonnage carried on the canal actually increased to such an extent that the reduction in the tolls did not affect the revenue earned. Thus the immediate result of railway ownership was not a transfer of trade away from the canal even though the railway had reached Maynooth by 1847 and Mullingar by 1848.

Rate of Completion of Midland Great Western Railway From 1847-1848.[7]

Points of completion adjoining the Royal Canal.	Date of Completion
Ashtown, county Dublin	1847
Clonsilla, county Dublin.	1847
Leixlip, county Kildare	1847
Maynooth, county Kildare	1847
Kilcock, county Kildare	1847
Enfield, county Meath	1847
Moyvalley, county Meath	1847
Killucan, county Westmeath	1848
Mullingar, county Westmeath	1848

The only surviving records of what was carried on the canal immediately after 1851 are three trade ledgers which show the quantities of commodities carried; they also show the destinations of the goods carried. These records show that business on the canal remained high until 1866. The only item to transfer completely to the railway was butter: 3,997 casks were carried on the canal between 12 October 1853 and 21 November 1853[8] but after this date, no further record of butter being carried is to be found and the assumption must be made that from the latter date, it was transported by railway.

Because of the size of these ledgers it was not possible to itemise each entry. In an attempt to analyse the quantities of goods carried between January 1854 and December 1866 samples of entries were taken from the three trade ledgers. In an effort to achieve a uniform sample over the twelve year period, three days, the 5th, 15th and 25th of every month were selected for each month of 1854, 1860 and 1866. This sample revealed that the same type of goods continued to be carried as in previous years although the carriage of live animals appears to have diminished greatly. A small number of pigs, for example, is recorded as being carried in 1854 compared with 18,607 in 1833 and 39,530 in 1834.[9] The samples taken for 1860 show that the quantities of goods carried increased during this period compared with 1854 with the exception of potatoes which decreased. The small tonnage of potatoes being carried reflected the farming trends of the period. Between 1855 and 1864 the acreage under tillage in Ireland fell from 4,276,954 to 3,765,059 acres and this trend continued up to 1870. Labour was scarce due to the famine and to heavy emigration and this contributed to the decline in the heavily labour intensive potato crop.[10]

The sample for 1866 shows a decline in the quantities of most goods being carried. It is also worth noting that the frequency of barges operating on the canal in 1866 was also reduced, with several days of the week where no traffic was recorded. The only commodity to record an increase in quantity being carried in 1866 was timber, with all such cargoes being deposited at the Liffey. As alterations were completed in 1867 by the railway company to Spencer Dock close to the Liffey, it is likely that the timber as well as stone which was also deposited in large quantities at the Liffey during this period were used in the building work.

The geographical pattern of flow of goods along the canal from 1854 to 1866 forms a definite pattern. Turf was carried in 1854 from Carrick-on-Shannon, Rooskey, Annaduce Bog, Tinnelick and Cappagh Bog to Dublin and this pattern remains until 1866. Manure was always carried from Dublin to such places as Leixlip and Maynooth but never further than Cappagh Bog. Similarly almost all general merchandise was carried from Dublin

Reduced Table of Tolls, Wharfage, &c.; and also Rates of Freight chargeable on the

ROYAL CANAL.

ARTICLES	Rate per Ton per mile (s. d.)	TOLLS AND FREIGHT CHARGEABLE BY BOAT OWNERS: To or from	Miles	Toll (s. d.)	Toll & Freight to be charged by Boat Owners (s. d.)
CORN, MEAL, FLOUR, POTATOES, BUTTER, BRAN, RAPESEED, BACON, BEEF, PORK, and all other Articles not hereinafter enumerated, at a rate not exceeding	0 1	RYE-AQUEDUCT ...	11	0 11	1 10
		MAYNOOTH	15	1 3	2 6
		KILCOCK ...	19	1 7	3 2
		FERNS 17th LOCK ...	22	1 10	3 8
		NEWCASTLE ...	27	2 3	4 6
		MOYVALLEY ...	31	2 7	5 2
		BOYNE AQUEDUCT ...	33	2 9	5 6
		BLACK SHADE ...	34	2 10	5 8
		HILL OF DOWN ...	36	3 0	6 0
		THOMASTOWN ...	42	3 2	6 4
		DOWN'S BRIDGE ...	47	3 4	6 8
		MULLINGAR ...	52	3 9	7 6
		BALLINEA ...	56	4 0	8 0
		COOLNAHAY ...	59	4 3	8 6
		BALLNACARIG ...	64	4 6	9 0
		ABBEYSHRUEL ...	70	5 0	10 0
		TENELICK ...	71	5 0	10 0
		BALLYMAHON ...	75	5 3	10 6
		TERLIKEN ...	78	5 6	11 0
		KENAGH ...	81	5 6	11 0
		KILLASHEE ...	87	5 9	11 6
		RICHMOND HARBOUR and LONGFORD	90	5 10	11 8

ARTICLES	Rate per Ton per mile (s. d.)	OBSERVATIONS.
MILL DUST	0 1	Not to exceed 2s. 6d. per Ton, if loaded with no other Article
SALT	0 1	Not to exceed 3s. per Ton, if loaded with no other Article.
HAY, STRAW (if loaded with no other Article) ...	0 1	Not to exceed 1s. 6d. per Ton for any distance.
Black CATTLE and SHEEP	0 1	Not exceeding 2s. 6d. per Ton.
PIGS, 2s. 6d. per Ton ...	...	But not a lesser sum than £1 10s. to be paid for a load or part of a load, for any distance.
BAGGAGE and MILITARY STORES	0 1	On any part of the Canal. With an escort of five Soldiers free. Any additional number of Soldiers, their Wives, and Children exceeding ten years of age, to be charged one farthing per mile for each person. Children under ten years of age to be free of charge.
DRAINAGE TILES ...	0 1	Not to exceed 1s. 6d. per Ton.
COAL	0 1	Not to exceed 1s. 8d. per Ton for any distance.
BRICKS	0 1	Not to exceed 10d. per Ton do.
TURF	0 1	Not to exceed 1s. per Ton do.
" CAPPAGH ...	0 1	Not to exceed 10d. per Ton, but not less than 40s. to be paid for a load or part of a load.
" from the Liffey, to or towards the Broadstone, 1s. per Ton.		
MANURE, TURF MOULD, or SAND	0 1	Not to exceed 18s. 6d. per Boat load for any distance.
STONES	0 1	Not to exceed 15s. per Boat load do.
MILL-STONES, FLAGS, MOUNTAIN GRANITE, CUT or HAMMERED Do.	0 1	Not to exceed 1s. 8d. per Ton.
GRAVEL, SHINGLING, & LIME	0 1	Not to exceed 4d. per Ton.—Gravel or Shingles taken from the Company's Banks, to pay 2d. per Ton value in addition to the Toll.
FLAGS, KELP, GYPSUM for making Plaster of Paris, Iron-stone and Slates, from the Shannon	0 1	Not to exceed 1s. per Ton. Gypsum is to be had in great abundance at Athlone.
PIG IRON, from ditto ...	0 1	Not to exceed 1s. 8d. per Ton, brought from Lough Allen with no other Article.

THE SHANNON TRADE.

	s. d.
ALL GOODS conveyed by the Royal Canal and the River Shannon, to or from Lanesborough, or any place South of the Canal, and North of Lough Rea, per Ton	5 0
ALL GOODS conveyed by the Royal Canal and the River Shannon, to or from Athlone, or any place Southward thereof, per Ton	5 0
GRAIN from Rooskey, Drumsna, Carrick-on-Shannon, or any Port upon the Shannon, North of Tarmonbarry, per Ton	5 0
FLOUR or OATMEAL, from any Port upon the Shannon, North of Lough Rea, Tarmonbarry excepted, per Ton	5 0
MERCHANDISE to Rooskey, Drumsna, Carrick-on-Shannon, or any Port upon the Shannon, North of Tarmonbarry, per Ton	5 0
COAL, TURF, and STONE, loaded upon the Shannon, and conveyed from thence to Longford, per Ton ...	0 6

DOCKAGE.

For the use of a Graving-Dock at Dublin, Mullingar, or Richmond Harbour, per day	5 0

WHARFAGE.

Round Timber, Rubble-Stone, Broken-Stone, or Manure remaining on the Company's Wharfs or Quays, exceeding Six Days after landing, to pay Three Shillings per week, or part of a week.

BRICKS, or any other articles landed at the Brick Quay or Broadstone, for every Boat load, or part of ditto...	5 0
TURF, for every Boat unloaded upon any part of the Line between the Liffey and Maynooth	5 0
MANURE, for every Cargo loaded at any of the Company's Quays, Wharfs, or Banks	2 6
On all Goods boated from the Liffey, and unloaded on the Liffey line, for every Boat load, or part of ditto...	10 0
On any Boat entering Richmond Harbour, from the Shannon, and there unloading	5 0

EMPTY BOATS.

For five miles, not going through a Lock	1 0
For any distance exceeding five miles, or going through a Lock	2 6
For twenty miles, or any greater distance	5 0

UNEMPLOYED BOATS.

For each and every day exceeding Fourteen Days a Boat remains unemployed at any of the Company's Harbours, Quays, or Wharfs, or within half a mile thereof	0 3

REGULATIONS RESPECTING CARGOES.

The whole Cargo being Potatoes, the toll not to exceed 2s. 6d. per Ton; or when a Boat is first partly loaded with Potatoes, and then Corn or other Articles loaded therein, the Toll not to exceed 2s. 6d. per Ton upon the Potatoes so loaded, provided the depths of the Boat have been distinctly ascertained by an Officer of the Company previously to her receiving the additional loading; but all Potatoes loaded after the depths have been taken in the manner above mentioned, are to pay One Penny per Ton per mile.

Boats loaded with Lime-Stone and Empty Hogsheads, conveyed from Richmond Harbour, or any Station upon the Line, to Dublin, chargeable wi[illegible] [illegible] per the entire Cargo.

Each Trader loading or discharging Commodities paying different Rates of Tolls, to produce a manifest of the Cargo in proper form, signed by the Boat Owner, and to give Notice to the Collector or other Officer to examine the respective depths, or, on failure, to be charged for the entire the highest Rate of any Commodity on Board; and an Affidavit to be made when required, to satisfy the Officer of the correctness of each transaction.—And in case Fraud or an attempt at Fraud shall be committed by false Manifests or otherwise, the full Toll will be charged on the entire Cargo, and one-half of Toll paid to any person detecting the same.

Any person reporting the particulars of any fraud committed upon the Company's Revenues, shall be entitled to one-half of the fine that may, in consequence thereof, be imposed,—or

Any person giving such information as will procure the conviction of any person that may be guilty of injuring Corn, or other Articles, or Pillaging Goods carried upon the Navigation, shall be liberally rewarded.

CHARGES ON MASTED VESSELS.

	£	s.	d.
On all descriptions of Goods to or from the River Liffey, loaded or unloaded in the Royal Docks, toll per Ton, per Register	0	0	0½
On such Masted Vessels leaving the Dock an additional charge of	0	1	0
For safe lying in the Dock a charge per ton, per register, Weekly	0	0	0½

By Order,

Broadstone, September, 1856.

HENRY BEAUSIRE, Secretary.

Figure 22: Table of Tolls, Wharfage and Rates of Freight on the Royal Canal, 1856.

and was distributed along the full length of the canal and on to the Shannon as far as Rooskey, Carrick-on-Shannon and Lanesborough. Coal was also carried from Dublin and distributed along the full length of the canal and on the Shannon, but the majority of coal was carried to Mullingar.

The largest volume of cargo transported on the canal during this period was corn and meal. Because the Trade Ledgers do not distinguish between these items, it is not possible to give separate tonnage for each. Although there is a reduction recorded in 1866 the trade in corn and meal appears to have remained buoyant. The majority of corn and meal was carried both to and from west of Mullingar. Because of the location of mills situated close to the canal at Archies Bridge and Tinnelick, county Longford and the diversion of the railway line away from the canal beyond Mullingar, the quantities of corn and meal carried on this section remained high. The net revenue earned by the canal which would have included tolls and rents was as follows: 1864/5 - £11,439, 1865/6 - £10,681, 1866/7 - £9,794[11] making an average for the three years of £10,638.

During this period a transfer of traffic from the canal to the railway was taking place but it was rather slow. The reduction of tolls in 1845 continued to allow the canal to be competitive, despite its close proximity to the railway and its lower speed. In 1867 in an effort to narrow the gap between railway and canal rates and to expedite the transfer of canal traffic to the railway, the railway company applied to have the canal tolls increased. Intervention by the Board of Control caused the application to be refused by the Lord Lieutenant on the grounds that the railway company had acquired the canal relatively cheaply and that in the public interest, the present rates of tolls charged should remain.

It is important to recall that at this time, the carriage of goods on the canal was undertaken by a number of boat owners who paid tolls to the railway company. The failure to have these tolls increased was what most probably prompted the railway company to establish themselves as carriers on the canal in 1870.[12] The establishment of additional boats on the canal when trade was diminishing might seem unusual but the railway company presumably intended to capture trade from the existing boat owners and eventually ruin their businesses which would leave the railway company with a monopoly.

Until 1876 an unknown number of railway owned horse drawn barges were used. In that year, the service was expanded when four new screw propelled boats were purchased at a cost of £5,000.[13] Yet, these developments failed to gain the monopoly hoped for by the railway company and the service was withdrawn in 1886 due to its unprofitability. The introduction of railway company vessels damaged the existing private boat owners and although they continued to operate on the canal their numbers fell from forty-four operating seventy-eight boats in 1866 to thirty-four operating forty-five boats in 1883.

In an attempt to gain more control over the affairs of the canal, the railway company had a bill presented to parliament in 1877 in which they tried to abolish the right of veto possessed by the Lord Lieutenant and the Board of Control over rates. Once again, the bill was opposed by the Board of Control and subsequently it was not passed. However an amendment was allowed in 1879 whereby the railway company could increase the toll for empty boats plying more than twenty miles on the canal. The railway company was also permitted to fill in part of the wharfage area at Broadstone Harbour in order to provide a forecourt for the railway terminus on condition that a new quay and turning place was provided for boats using the Broadstone branch. The railway company had in fact operated a station at Broadstone from as early as 1847[14] but what arrangements were in place to facilitate passengers prior to 1850 are not known. A railway station was erected on a site ajoining the canal harbour in 1850 and passengers and vehicular traffic crossed the harbour by means of a floating pontoon to gain access to the railway station.

Figure 23: Broadstone Railway Station, built by the Midland Great Western Railway c. 1850.

The docks where the canal entered the river Liffey as proposed in 1790 by the Royal Canal Company were never completed, although they appear on maps of the period. Rather, this section of canal appears to have had nothing more than ordinary canal bank wharfage, with access to the river Liffey[15] suitable for canal barges only but these facilities together with those at Broadstone Harbour seem to have been adequate, given the quantities of goods which were being carried on the canal. However, they became totally inadequate to handle railway traffic as the railway served a much larger hinterland.

Boats and Names of Owners using the Royal Canal
1866[16]

Owner	Number of Boats	Owner	Number of Boats
McDonnell	1	Butler	4
Finley	1	Shaw	2
Kelly	7	McCann	4
Murtagh	7	Clarke	3
Doyle	1	Cahill	1
Coyne	7	Sullivan	1
Bray	1	Levey	1
Commins	1	Slevin	1
Caffrey	1	Kilmurray	1
Murphy	1	McGuire	2
Todd	1	Beatty	1
Kenny	2	Garvey	2
Farrell	2	Campbell	1
Hayden	1	Lynch	1
Byrne	1	Connolly	1
McCormick	1	Kenny	1
Dunne	3	Larverty	1
Commins	1	Freeman	1
Nugent	1	Fleming	1
Flood	1	Marrow	1
Finley	1	Murray	1
Murray	1	Fullam	1
Lannery	1	Total	78

Boats, and Names of Owners using the Royal Canal
1883 and 1892[17]

Owner	1883	1892
Durkin	3	1
McCann	3	–
Caffery	1	1
Shaw	2	–
Levey	2	1
McDonnell	2	2
Buckley	1	–
Garvey	1	–
Byrne	2	1
Farrell	1	1
Mooney	1	–
Mitchell	1	–
Boyham	–	1
Fee	–	2
Devery	–	1
Cokely	–	1
Murphy	–	1
Fitzsimons	1	–
Kennedy	2	2
Roe	5	–
Lannery	1	1
Kelly	1	1
Fleming	4	3
Doyle	1	–
Dunne	1	1
N.C.M.Co.	7	5
Walsh	1	–
Connell	1	–
McNeill	1	–
Leech	–	1
Carroll	–	1
Hayes	–	1
Hughes	–	1
Daris	–	1
Total	45	31

Schedule of Tolls and Wharfage for Empty Boats passing along the Royal Canal 1879.[18]

		s - d
Empty boats travelling any distance not exceeding five miles and not passing through a lock.		1 - 0
Empty boats travelling any distance not exceeding five miles but passing through a lock.		2 - 6
Empty boats exceeding five miles but under twenty miles and not passing through a lock.		2 - 6
Empty boats any distance exceeding five miles and under twenty miles passing through a lock.		4 - 0
For empty boats travelling more than twenty miles		6 - 0
Empty boats remaining at a harbour or wharf or within a quarter mile of same for more than four days.	per day	0 - 3
Cost of using graving dock per day		7 - 6
Goods remaining on wharfs or harbours exceeding one week charged per ton.	per day	0 - 4

In 1867, improvements were completed by the railway company to Spencer Dock. The wharfage accommodation was extended and railway facilities were provided on both sides. The sea lock was left unaltered.[19]

In 1873 further major renovations were carried out. Spencer Dock now covered two acres and had one thousand seven hundred and forty yards of quay frontage. The sea lock was also altered at this time allowing the passage of small coastal vessels capable of carrying up to five hundred tons of cargo into the dock with a view to connecting directly with the railway and the canal.

An Increase in Tolls and Further Decline

Figure 24: Spencer Dock built by Midland Great Western Railway in 1867 and extended in 1873.

In 1881 at the request of the railway company an enquiry was held at Dublin Castle into the tolls being levied on the canal traffic.[20] As a result, it was recommended that the tolls be increased. As on previous occasions, the increase was opposed by the Board of Control. By now, the condition of the canal had deteriorated and numerous complaints were being received by the Board from traders and these were used as the basis for their objections. The objections were overruled and new tolls requested by the Railway Commissioners were accepted by the Lord Lieutenant as the maximum tolls which could be levied.

The increases did not affect all items carried. Selected goods which were generally carried in bulk had their tolls increased. The toll on slates was increased from 1s-0d[21] maximum to 3s-9d maximum from Dublin to Mullingar. Similarly bricks were increased from 10d to 1s-0d per ton per mile and hay and straw from 1s-6d to 2s-0d per ton per mile. Items such as sand and gravel could be carried any distance at a cost not to exceed 9d per ton per mile or, alternatively, a boatload of gravel could be carried any distance for 18s-9d and sand for £1-3s-0d.[22] It emerged later that the boatload rate was charged regardless of how much was carried.[23]

No figures exist to show the quantities of goods being carried between Dublin and Mullingar in 1881. Because many of the increased tolls applied to this section of the canal, it must be assumed that a considerable trade continued between these two centres and that the railway directors worked to cause a transfer of canal trade to the railway.

As a result of the increased tolls the margin between the rate for railway carriage and canal carriage narrowed and consequently transporting goods by the canal became less competitive. It must be recalled that the payment of the appropriate canal toll merely allowed a boat to pass along the canal and was only a portion of the overall rate charged. Wages, the feeding of horses and profit for the boat operator were the other elements which made up the full freight rate.

The increase in tolls meant that the boat owners were now faced with the dilemma of either adding the increased tolls to their overall rate thus becoming uncompetitive or of absorbing the extra tolls thereby reducing their profits. Tolls on the return journey of an empty boat if no cargo was found, which was a regular occurrence during this period, greatly affected the earnings of the boat owners. In contrast to the canal traders, the railway company had no tolls to pay. The rate charged for transport by railway included loading, unloading and carriage to the destination.

There is no doubt that the railway company would have liked to have closed down the canal. However, the powers of control granted to the Board of Control in the Act of Parliament in 1845 and the conditions under which the railway company bought the canal made it impossible to achieve this legally. It must, therefore, be assumed that a conscious decision was taken by the directors of the railway to kill the trade on the canal by whatever means available and this was achieved in a number of ways. First, canal tolls were increased to a level where it became impossible for the boat owners to operate in competition with the railway. Second, railway rates were sometimes reduced. Prior to the general increase in tolls in 1881, certain commodities such as grain had been traditionally carried in large quantities on the canal. In 1876, for example, the toll on grain from Longford to Dublin was 5s-10d per ton compared with the railway rate of 11s-8d per ton. In order to divert the grain traffic from barge to railway, the railway company reduced the rate for the carriage of grain by train from 11s-8d to 4s-0d per ton on seven ton loads and thus captured the bulk of the grain trade from county Longford and the Shannon region.

After 1881, the introduction of the new tolls plus a deterioration in the condition of the canal due to lack of maintenance caused trade to go into a rapid decline. Between 1883 and 1892, the number of boats operating on the canal declined from forty-five to thirty-one. The tonnage carried also declined considerably. In 1883, the revenue received from tolls and wharfage was less than expenditure on maintenance and operation.

Deterioration of the Canal's Physical Condition

Apart from the high tolls, the physical condition of the canal seriously affected trading. It had begun to deteriorate soon after it was taken over in 1845 due to lack of proper maintenance. The Board of Control although appointed to ensure that the canal would remain operational had never been allocated permanent engineering staff.[24]

Return of Tonnage carried on the Royal Canal,
and amount of Tolls on same,
from 1 January to 31 December, 1883[25]

Description of Goods	Weight Tons	Tolls and Wharfage Amount £-s-d
Sand, Clay, Stones	12,315	219-13-3
Bricks, Flags	1,224	38- 8-6
Manure, Bog Stuff	3,488	89- 1-3
Coal	11,609	704- 6-2
Turf	1,290	66- 6-8
Pit Wood, Native Timber	2,203	219- 4-1
Grain, Flour, Meal, Sundries	13,482	1,758-13-2
Empty Boats	—	127-16-6
Total	45,611	3,223- 9-7

Expenditure on the Royal Canal 1883 - 1893[26]

	Years				
	1883 £	1890 £	1891 £	1892 £	1893 £
Maintenance					
Wages	2,420	2,371	2,507	2,501	2,432
Materials	818	496	343	284	309
Lock Keepers' Wages	1,174	1,014	1,010	1,028	1,010
Rates and Taxes	248	391	252	445	218
Miscellaneous	48	24	43	41	68
Total	4,708	4,296	4,155	4,299	4,037

In June 1878, an application was made by the Board of Control to the government for permanent engineering staff to be appointed to supervise the canal. The rejection of this application instigated a request from the Board for the temporary appointment of an engineer until improvements were made. Legal advice sought on the matter revealed that no provision was made in the Act of 1818 or in subsequent Acts for the appointment of staff to the Board. Thus the situation was that the Board of Control had power to inspect the canal and to insist that maintenance and work be carried out to ensure that the canal remained navigable, but it had no staff to carry out or supervise this work.

Because of increased public funding during this period, engineers employed by the Commissioners of Public Works were under extreme pressure. In 1883 parliament passed the Tramways and Public Companies Act which led to the construction of seven new narrow gauge railway lines.[27] In 1886 and 1889, Light Railway Acts were passed resulting in twelve more lines being constructed. Work was also in progress on the River Shannon Drainage Scheme and improvements were being made to many harbours and piers throughout the country. The advent of this work necessitated surveys, involving hundreds of miles, to be carried out by the engineers of the Commissioners of Public Works, leaving no time to deal with such projects as the Royal Canal.

Although the Board of Control was still the statutory body involved in monitoring the canal. It ceased to operate effectively after 1885. In that year two members resigned[28] and were not replaced until 1906. Because the Board ceased to exercise proper supervision over the canal, complaints from traders and boat owners were now directed at the Board of Trade.[29] In 1888-9 extensive powers were acquired by this Board: in effect, although they had no legal right to intervene in the affairs of the canal, they assumed the role previously held by the Board of Control.

In 1894 due to the large number of complaints received about the condition of the canal, an enquiry was held under the direction of the Board of Trade. Recommendations made by Major General Hutchinson, who had inspected the canal, were not implemented by the railway. As Major Hutchinson's report was not published it is not known what his recommendations were. However it emerged later that sections of the canal at that stage had only three feet of water. No maintenance[30] had been carried out for the previous ten years.

The refusal of the railway to carry out the recommended repairs led to a further inquiry which was held in 1895 and a more detailed survey was carried out by Major Marindin.[31] This investigation revealed that the canal was in a very bad state. From Mullingar to Longford the situation was particularly poor: small trees were growing from the bank into the water. The condition of the towpaths was such that several horses had sustained broken legs because of the uneven surface. Almost the entire length of the canal was choked with weeds and extensive stretches, particularly under bridges and in locks, were heavily silted. The sluice gates at Lough Owel had rotted and water flowed continuously into the canal. A similar condition applied at the locks at the Liffey entrance: at the sea end water poured freely from the canal into the river. Consequently in dry summer weather the reservoir at Lough Owel was depleted and the canal ran dry.

Pressure from the government in view of Marindin's report forced the railway company to begin a maintenance programme[32] on the canal. In 1896, a dredger was purchased to remove the silt, and weed-cutting crews were employed to remove the weeds and keep the banks in repair. While some maintenance was carried out, progress was slow and only half-hearted. The weeds were cut just below the surface of the water and placed on the bank. Similarly silt removed from the canal was also placed on top of the bank. The result was that in times of heavy rain both were washed back into the canal.[33] By

1905, boats which had a capacity to carry seventy tons, were, because of the weeds and lack of water, only able to carry thirty tons or less. The number of boats operating on the canal in that year was reduced to twenty-two and subsequently the year's tolls were only £2,304.

In 1905, the railway company applied to the Board of Trade for permission to abandon the Broadstone branch of the canal. A decision was not made immediately. In 1906, a Royal Commission on Canals and Waterways looked into the condition of all canals in the British Isles. As input to this exercise, the Board of Control of the Royal Canal commissioned Dudley Fletcher, an employee of the Board of Works and Inspector of the Shannon Navigation to report on the condition of the canal. He reported that from Richmond Harbour to Killashee, the canal was choked with weeds and almost impassable as was the Longford branch. From the 1st to the 5th locks, boats could not get within seventeen feet of the banks to unload their cargo. Considerable leakage was occurring at many of the lock gates. An apparent effort had been made to rectify the leakage at Lough Owel.

It was the opinion of the Commission[34] having received Fletcher's report that the railway company had utilised the Royal Canal for its own interests and subsequently that it was in a very neglected condition. With regard to the 1905 application to close the Broadstone branch, it was recommended that this be refused, the view being that Broadstone Harbour was required as terminal facilities for the canal. The Commission further recommended that if the canal remained in the possession of the railway company, the company should seek special parliamentary powers if it still wished to abandon the branch.[35]
Although the number of traders operating boats on the canal in 1905 remained the same as in 1892 the number of boats decreased from thirty-one to twenty-two. Between 1901 and 1905 only a small decrease is recorded in the amount of tolls and wharfage collected from the canal, indicating that during this period the quantities of goods available for carriage remained the same, but were carried by fewer boats.

List of Boatowners Trading on the Canal - 1905.[36]

Owner	No. of Boats
C.R. Carriage	2
Kirpatrick, Kilcock	1
North City Mills, Dublin	4
William Lenocks, Mullingar	1
James Byrne, Abbeyshrule	1
Thomas Byrne, Agher, Enfield	1
John Coffey, operated between Grand and Royal Canals.	1
McGingan-Smith	1
Patrick Doyle, Kilcock	2
Joseph Leech, Dublin	2
Mrs. Reilly, Kilcock	2
William Leech, Killucan	2
Thomas McLoughlin, Longford	1
Gordon, Grand Canal Boat	1
	22

Revenue for Tolls and Wharfage on Royal Canal 1901-1905[37]

Year	Tolls, Wharfages	Rents	Total
1901	2,684	2,594	5,278
1902	2,562	2,416	4,978
1903	2,166	2,406	4,572
1904	2,477	2,424	4,900
1905	2,304	2,451	4,716

The Final Years

The recommendations of the 1906 Royal Commission were never implemented nor was the Broadstone branch officially closed although it did fall into disuse. In 1923,

Figure 25: Abandoned canal barge at Spencer Dock.

when Dáil Éireann set up the Canals and Waterways Commission the condition of the canal had deteriorated further. The number of traders had been reduced to twelve.[38] Tolls which had been increased in 1894[39] were further increased in 1920[40] by one hundred and twenty per cent. These increases had a devastating effect. The principal items carried at this time were coal, flour, timber, bog-ore and a small amount of grain. Sand which had been carried in large quantities was now being transported by road at a more competitive rate.

When part of the wharfage area at Broadstone was closed in 1877, no replacement arrangements were made at the new Spencer Dock for the canal traders. Rather, the original stores built by the canal company were allowed to fall into disrepair, leaving traders with no place to store goods in the area. This was further complicated by the fact that whole wharfages in Spencer Dock were completely filled with coal[41] awaiting transport by railway leaving no area for storage of products using the canal boats.

By 1923, all the original stores on the canal route had been converted for railway use or rented for other purposes.[42] This lack of storage and wharfage facilities was another major contributing factor to ever declining trade. Thus, for example, the transport of bricks which were manufactured in large quantities in county Longford and sent to Dublin by canal was discontinued due to the lack of wharfage.[43] Items such as furniture and perishable goods also transferred from canal to railway for the same reason.[44]

In 1923 only one coal boat operated on the canal,[45] the majority of the coal going to Ballymahon, a point not served by railway. While considerable amounts of coal were used in other towns and villages along the canal route, the price of carriage by canal was uncompetitive: the rate on a ton of coal including the 3s-8d toll was 12s-0d while the rate by railway was only 11s-10d.[46] A rebate to the purchaser of 7d per ton was allowed on quantities of over one hundred and sixty tons carried by canal; the rebate on a similar tonnage transported by train was 2s-0d per ton. In addition, coal carried by the canal was charged wharfage while coal carried by train was exempt.

By 1923, Richmond Harbour had been closed to traffic and only one boat operated into Longford town.[47] The principal commodities carried in the early 1920s were sundries which consisted mainly of barrels of Guinness, coal, bog ore and round timber. The total income from tolls and rents in 1922 was £4,951 yielding a loss of £17,914.

Receipts and Expenditure of the Royal Canal
1914 and 1920 to 1922[48]

	1914 £	1920 £	1921 £	1922 £
Receipts				
Tolls and Charges	2,396	2,006	3,269	3,111
Rents	2,145	1,754	1,485	1,840
Total	4,541	3,760	4,754	4,951
Expenditure				
Superintendence	175	306	294	300
Lock keepers	906	4,816	4,518	3,555
Maintenance	4,947	11,158	13,751	11,605
Rates	487	697	863	834
Miscellaneous	15	563	570	6,571
Total	6,530	17,540	19,996	22,865
Loss on Working	1,989	13,780	15,242	17,914

There are no official records of how many boats operated or what was carried on the Royal Canal after 1923. However boats did continue on the canal in competition with the railway[49] after this date. Trade with the towns and villages east of Mullingar was very small and the boat owners depended on the towns and villages west of Mullingar where no railway stations existed, such as Ballynacarrigy, Keenagh and Ballymahon, for their business.

Up to 1923 the railway company was not allowed by law to operate road transport services.[50] When this restriction was removed, the railway company built up a fleet of lorries at the larger centres such as Mullingar and began to operate a door-to-door service to the towns not served directly by the railway. Thus it is most likely that after 1923 the numbers of traders operating on the canal began to diminish.

In 1925, twenty-six separate railway companies in the Irish Republic were amalgamated to form the Great Southern Railway Company (GSR).[51] The amalgamation was brought about by increased competition from motor transport and as a result of an almost threefold rise in labour costs over the pre-world war level. The Royal Canal thus became part of the GSR. The Transport Act of 1944 provided for the merger of the GSR and the Dublin United Tramway Company into a new organisation: Córas Iompair Éireann (CIE). The Royal Canal now became part of the even larger national transport system. In 1946 when Tom Rolt[52] navigated the Royal Canal, there were only two boats operating: Mr. Leech from Killucan, county Westmeath, and Mr. Caffery from Summerhill in Dublin. By 1951, this number had been reduced to one boat and trading on the canal ceased in July of that year when Leech's boat plied the canal for the last time.

The 1960 Transport Act[53] gave power to CIE to close the canal to navigation which it did on 6 April 1966. Almost immediately after this, CIE placed a dam across the canal at Ballinea three miles west of Mullingar thereby cutting off the main supply of water to points west. Certain local authorities were given permission to build low level bridges across the canal west of Mullingar.

Chapter Six

The Revival of the Royal Canal

After its closure in 1961 and the building of a dam at Ballinea (1964) most of the western section of the canal dried out and soon it was impossible to distinguish parts of the canal from the surrounding landscape. Although the eastern stretch remained in water it was little more than a linear swamp. There seemed at that time no future for the canal.

In 1953 the Inland Waterways Association (IWAI) was formed with a number of aims regarding our inland waterways. These included advancing the tourist amenities provided by our rivers and canals, opposing the abandonment of waterways and the imposition of any obstruction to their navigation. Over the years the group grew and was actively involved in the Shannon Navigation, river Barrow and the Grand Canal. A formal request to close the Grand Canal was forwarded by Dublin Corporation to the Minister for Local Government in November 1963.[1] The Corporation wished to use the bed of the canal where it circles the south of the city as a route for a surface water sewer. This would then have been concreted over, the new surface to be used as a roadway. This proposal prompted IWAI to mount a publicity campaign to prevent the closure. Leaflets were produced making a case for retaining the canal and for developing it as a tourist amenity. These leaflets were distributed widely and indicated the low cost of maintaining the waterways. It was stressed that income would improve if existing boat hire operators were allowed to develop their potential by being offered long-term secure leases. The IWAI carried out an intensive campaign to save the canal and the result was that Dublin Corporation agreed in 1969 to place the sewer in a tunnel beneath the canal.

In 1978 the government announced that the Grand Canal, the Royal Canal and the Barrow Navigation would be transferred from CIE ownership to the custody of the Office of Public Works (OPW). Although this did not happen at this time, the future of the inland navigation in the south of Ireland became brighter from this point on. The IWAI made plans to revive the Naas and Kilbeggan branches of the Grand Canal through local associations and by using voluntary labour. By March 1971, work was in progress on the Milltown feeder of the Grand Canal near Lowtown, county Kildare. This work was carried out by CIE staff with the aid of a grant from Bord Fáilte and the local council. To further enhance the area as a tourist attraction, a local group of canal enthusiasts restored and ran the old Canal Hotel at Robertstown Harbour and also began to operate a boat for day trips on that section of the canal.

The Start of Restoration

Inspired by the efforts of those at Robertstown, an article by A. J. McEvoy appeared in *Canaliana* describing the condition of the Royal Canal.[2] An inspection of several lengths revealed that overall the masonry in the locks and bridges was still sound and that the water supply appeared copious despite many years of neglect. However the lock gates were in a sad state: only a few were restorable and most had long since ceased to retain the water levels in the various channels they served. In parts, nothing more than a trickle of water meandered through the rushes. Vegetation characteristic of dry land flourished throughout and the harbour at Kilcock resembled a linear swamp.

McEvoy put forward a plan to help stop this deterioration and to prevent what once was a broad smooth waterway becoming a dry ditch which would inevitably become a "dump for old cars and rejected household appliances". While he saw no immediate prospect of total restoration due to the enormous cost involved, he identified that the principal cause of the deterioration, was the failure to maintain water levels as various lock gates fell into decay. If resources were not available to replace the gates, he suggested the use of coffer dams or sheet piling placed in the canal bed above the locks. These would help to retain water at the various levels, establish an aquatic ecology between the banks of the canal and, most important, arrest further encroachment on them by vegetation. With this arrangement, the canal would recover much of its visual appearance and sports such as fishing and boating could be revived.

Although it was stated at a public meeting in Maynooth organised by An Taisce in 1970 that there was no reason why the canal could not be restored apart from the cost, it was not until 1974 that positive steps were taken towards restoration. It was proposed in *Inland Waterways News*[3] by Dr Ian Bath that a "group or federation to spearhead the protection and development of the Royal Canal" be formed. Support for this group was substantial and a paper was distributed outlining the condition of the canal and how complete restoration might be achieved.[4] In April 1974, the Royal Canal Amenity Group (RCAG) was founded by Ian Bath, with the specific aim of highlighting the amenity potential of a restored Royal Canal. Immediately, volunteer work parties started to clean up and clear sections of the line between Castleknock and Blanchardstown, county Dublin. Through negotiations between the group and CIE, it was agreed that some of the lock gates would be repaired by CIE staff. By cannibalising the middle gates of the 12th lock they "made good" the top gates. This resulted in the 7½ mile 12th level being restored to full depth.

Over the summer months of 1974, RCAG work parties operating in the evenings and at weekends cleared towpaths and the channel between Castleknock and Blanchardstown and in September when they published their first newsletter, *Royal Canal News* [5] it was reported that considerable progress had been made with the work and that it had been confirmed by CIE that obstructions to the canal which might be detrimental to its longer term restoration would not be allowed.

Support for the RCAG continued to grow throughout 1974-5. Their second newsletter of January 1975[6] reported restoration activities taking place at Enfield, Moyvalley, Leixlip, Maynooth and Mullingar. However many years were to elapse before RCAG branches were established in these towns. It also urged Westmeath County Council to "think again about their plans to culvert the canal at Shandonagh and Ballinea bridges" at Mullingar.

By the summer of 1975,[7] members of the RCAG with the help of venture scouts and Porterstown Youth Club cleared the tow path from the city boundary at Ratoath Road, Cabra (Reilly's Bridge) to Callahan Bridge, Clonsilla. At the same time, CIE began to cut weeds on this section and followed this up with treatment by weed killer to supress further growth. In June 1975, the RCAG members along with some local residents began to clean out the 10th lock and 9th level at Ashtown – the first such venture of its kind on the canal for many years. Dublin County Council provided machinery and lorries for the job and at the end of the first day's work, four lorry loads of rubbish and six old cars were removed. Similar amounts were removed on the following two Saturdays.

Although restoration work was in progress in and near Dublin, a threat of closure to the canal within the Dublin city boundary remained until 1976. In 1971, the Dublin Transportation Study[8] recommended that a road be built along the line of the Royal Canal from Castleknock to the North Strand, a distance of 5.8 miles. The Dublin Development Plan of 1971[9] shows this proposed route with another along the bed of the Grand Canal. The two routes were to direct vehicular traffic away from the inner city area and to provide direct access to Dublin port.[10]

By 1976, the proposed Royal Canal route had been modified;[11] the line of the canal from Ashtown to the North Strand Road was now designated for conservation. However the section from Spencer Dock to the river Liffey was still to be incorporated into a north-south eastern bypass. Completion of this proposal would in effect sever communication between the river Liffey and the Royal Canal. Although this threat remained, the voluntry work continued in the hope that the problem could be resolved at some later stage.

The First Comprehensive Plan for Re-Development

On 30 November 1978, the then Minister for Tourism and Transport, Mr. Padraig Faulkner announced[12] that the government had given approval for the transfer of the Royal Canal to the OPW. He stated "that the Royal Canal is to be developed as resources permit by carrying out improvement works on selected stretches. The nature and financing of the works involved would be a matter for discussion between the Office of Public Works and Bord Fáilte and, where appropriate, local authorities and voluntary organisations."

In the light of this announcement, a restoration plan for the Royal Canal was prepared by the IWAI[13] and distributed to interested parties such as the Office of Public Works, Bord Fáilte, the local authorities and voluntary and sporting organisations concerned with canal-based activities such as angling and canoeing. The aim of the wide circulation was to secure joint agreement and action by all the interested parties in order to bring about the restoration of the canal as quickly as possible.

The RCAG had been carrying out improvement works as previously described, but the extent of their activities had been restricted by the uncertainty regarding the future of the canal. The government announcement in 1978 clarified the situation and was seen as giving the green light for more extensive restoration work with the ultimate objective of fully restoring the canal to navigation. No major impediments existed to fulfilling this objective; the line of the canal was intact throughout, and the only major obstacles were culverted and low bridge road crossings in Mullingar and in county Longford.

The IWAI plan set out in detail the overall condition of the canal in 1979 and the work required to be done to restore it, initially as a useful amenity and eventually as a navigation possessing high recreational and tourism potential. It was hoped that the plan would be accepted as a discussion document and as a means by which local authorities and voluntary organisations could devise a programme of preliminary improvement works for selected stretches to be carried out during the rest of 1979 and 1980. The overall objective of the IWAI plan was to bring about the restoration of the Royal Canal as a navigable waterway, to set out the work involved and to recommend the order in which this should be completed. The restoration of the canal as a navigable waterway did not involve any insurmountable engineering problems. As the Minister's announcement of 30 November 1978 envisaged, co-operation between the OPW and the local authorities, as well as Bord Fáilte and voluntary organisations, was essential as the work to be done was considered on a county by county basis. Although it was understood that it would take a number of years to fully restore the canal, it was hoped that major recreational benefits would accrue as the work progressed.

Restoration 1977-1984

In 1977 RCAG and the Dublin Branch of IWAI set about making a new breast gate for the 13th lock near Leixlip, county Kildare. On three evenings per week for about one year the volunteers worked on the project in Lucan vocational school. Timber was supplied free by timber merchants, Mallinsons of Swords, county Dublin. Unfortunately after the gate was fitted and the lock filled the sheeting on the north tailgate burst making through passage impossible. Undaunted the RCAG carried on. Again in 1977 they applied to CIE for permission to restore the 14th, 15th, 16th and 17th locks but permission was declined mainly because it was considered to be pre-empting the decision of the Minister for Tourism and Transport regarding the future of the canal. However, in 1980 after another approach was made to the Department

Plate 5: (top) The 16th lock at Kilcock before restoration, 1981.
(bottom) The 36th lock at Ballynacarrigy before restoration, 1981

of Tourism and Transport regarding the restoration of the locks, permission was granted.[14] While it was hoped that part of the cost, which was estimated at £12,000 for the materials, would be met by an amenity grant from both Kildare and Meath county councils it was expected that the majority of the money would have to be raised by the RCAG themselves.

While the clearing of towpaths and the cleaning of the waterway and locks referred to already contributed enormously to the local amenity value of the canal in certain areas, such as between Cross Guns Bridge and Binns Bridge in Dublin, the overall restoration effort was still hampered in 1979 by the condition of most of the lock gates. In an attempt to overcome this situation, the RCAG set about acquiring premises in which to manufacture lock gates. With AnCo trainees making the gates and financial help from Dublin Corporation to cover the cost of timber to make a set of gates for the 3rd lock at Whitworth Road, Drumcondra, the project got underway and by October 1980, premises were leased gratis on an annual basis from Guinness Ireland. These were located at Watling Street and were officially inaugurated by Mr. Albert Reynolds T.D. then Minister for Transport as the Watling Street Lock Gate Factory on 26 February 1981.

By 1983, the lock gate factory had produced gates for the 2nd and 3rd locks in Dublin city, for the 11th and 12th locks at Blanchardstown and for the 13th lock beyond Leixlip, county Kildare. A pair of gates were also manufactured for the 26th lock at Coolnahay, county Westmeath, which enabled a ten mile stretch of canal to be re-watered through Ballynacarrigy and Abbeyshrule. These gates also made it possible to remove the dam at Ballinea. By January 1984, thirty sets of gates had been manufactured at Watling Street for the Royal Canal while a further six had been made for the Naas branch of the Grand Canal.

A chance meeting between Michael Clinton and Eddie Slane, Chairman of RCAG at Kilcock Harbour in 1982 led to the setting up of a branch of the RCAG in the area. Soon work was started on the restoration of the harbour which adjoins the main N4 Road to the west. By 1984, this work was well in hand and restoration of the 16th level above the harbour had begun.

With the success of the group at Kilcock, RCAG branches were formed at Enfield, Maynooth, Longwood, Thomastown and Leixlip. By the end of 1984, RCAG work parties were restoring the canal at various sections in Dublin and county Dublin, at Maynooth, county Kildare, Enfield, county Meath, and at Killucan, Mullingar and Ballynacarrigy, county Westmeath. While the majority of the work from 1979 to 1984 was concentrated on the eastern section, work on small parts of the western section was also undertaken. In 1980, a mile of canal was cleared of trees and bushes at Abbeyshrule, county Longford, by the Abbeyshrule-Ballynacarrigy branch which was formed in 1978. Stop planks were positioned at Webb's Bridge in the village and at Quinn's Bridge near Abbeyshrule airfield in order to enable this section of canal to be filled with water. Most of the water for this section came from the Balroe feeder. Although a plentiful supply was to be had in winter, the water was scarce during the summer months.

In November 1984, the RCAG submitted proposals to Dublin County Council for financial assistance to repair and renew lock gates in the county Dublin section. It was estimated that this work would cost £49,000 and Dublin County Council responded immediately and granted £10,000 towards the work. This enabled work to commence on gates for the 11th lock and for repairs to the wing wall of Talbot Bridge to be completed. The 12th lock was cleared and landscaped.

The takeover of the canal by the OPW in July 1986 and the prospect of its eventual complete restoration helped to ease the financial problems of the RCAG which was now working with the blessing of the OPW. However in small communities along the route, fund-raising by every possible means was still the usual means of obtaining

Plate 6: (top) Kilcock Harbour before restoration, 1982.
(bottom) Kilcock Harbour after restoration, 1986.

Plate 7: (top) The harbour at Ballynacarrigy before restoration, 1982.
(bottom) The restored harbour at Ballynacarrigy, 1985.

finance for developing sections of the canal. In order to build a slipway at Thomastown Harbour, county Westmeath and to restore water to the 20th level which had been dry for some years, volunteers from the Killucan branch of the RCAG held a Christmas morning sponsored swim which raised £400 and two musical evenings in a local pub which added a further £600. Trees, rubbish and weeds were cleared and plastic sheeting was placed over the lock gates which enabled the level to be re-watered on a trial basis. This re-watering was successful, with only a little seepage through the south bank.

Problems with seepage in stretches which had been dry for some time were frequently encountered during the restoration. The most common causes were found to be cracking of the puddle (clay) lining of the bed and banks due to drying up, burrows made in the banks by animals and holes made by tree roots.

Like Killucan, other small communities continued to work on the stretches of the Royal Canal which passed through their areas. At the end of December 1984, dredging work which had been abandoned some years previously due to lack of funds, recommenced on the harbour at Ballynacarrigy, county Westmeath. To carry out the work, the harbour and the level above it were drained allowing machinery to clear the silt in the harbour. While the work was in progress, the stonework surrounding the harbour was repaired and repointed by local young people employed on a Youth Employment Scheme. The dam at Ballinea which was put in place in 1961 was also removed.

In Maynooth, county Kildare, a branch of the RCAG was formed in August 1984. In connection with this branch, an AnCo community youth training project was set up to restore the harbour and surrounding area. Initially five young people were employed, but by March 1985 the number had grown to eighteen. Preliminary work revealed that the harbour wall was in a very poor condition and in cases non-existent. Extensive rebuilding was required. The provision of a new boat slip was part of the proposed work. By 1987, a considerable amount of work had been completed. Over 10,000 tons of silt had been removed from the harbour and 140 metres of the harbour walls had been re-built on new foundations with plans to build similar walls at Bond Bridge. While work continued on the new slipway, the area around the harbour including the towpath was cleared and landscaped and new seating was provided. On Sunday 19 June 1988, thirty small boats sailed from Confey at Leixlip to Maynooth Harbour. These were the first craft to navigate this section for more than thirty years.

By 1985, the restoration work being undertaken by the RCAG had developed from removing rubbish from locks and short stretches of the canal to much more ambitious programmes aimed at full restoration. Machinery was now being hired for dredging longer lengths and, in particular, harbour areas. In Kilcock, for example, the local RCAG branch, again in conjunction with AnCo trainees, used hired machinery to clear silt and rubbish from the harbour area and the stretch of canal which runs parallel with the N4 Road as it enters the town. At one stage, this work was in danger of being abandoned because of the heavy expenditure involved and in an effort to continue, the branch decided to purchase their own equipment. Within a short time, a 10 R.B. drag-line excavator in need of considerable repair had been located in a sand quarry in county Wicklow and was purchased for £200. A further £300 was spent on parts and the excavator was restored to working order. By the end of March 1985 the branch had purchased from the OPW a second more powerful machine (22 R.B. drag-line) which was funded by AnCo.

Between 1985 and 1987, the stretch of canal in the Kilcock area was transformed from a swamp to a fully restored section. The harbour was cleaned and the level between it and the 15th lock was dredged. Chambers Bridge was restored and a major leak where the canal runs parallel with the main N4 Road was repaired. The harbour above and below the 16th lock was rebuilt and a leisure park was created between the railway line and the harbour with walkways on both sides of the canal.

Plate 8: (top) Boat Rally on the Royal Canal. Members of the Royal Canal Amenity Group leaving the 13th lock near Maynooth.
(bottom) Swans on the Royal Canal near Reilly's Bridge, Cabra.

As a result of the transformation of the canal in Kilcock, the local perception of the canal changed from viewing it as a nuisance and a public eyesore to seeing it as a local amenity of considerable value. Because of the restored waterway, an annual "Canal Week and Festival" has developed in the town, with activities ranging from the selection of a Canal Queen to road races and watersports.

In 1982, a small group of people from the local community in Enfield, county Meath, began to clear the banks of the canal and to plant trees and shrubs. The old harbour area situated a quarter of a mile south-west of the village was identified as being suitable for development as a leisure park. In 1984, a branch of RCAG was formally set up in the town to take over the task of restoration. The new branch operated under the umbrella of Enfield Community Council. Once again assistance was sought from AnCo and a scheme was commenced in conjunction with the RCAG employing twenty young local people and a supervisor. The work involved rebuilding the harbour walls, dredging, laying out paths and landscaping. By March 1985, much of this work was in progress including the demolition of the old harbour stores which were in a dangerous condition. On Sunday 28 June 1987 the Enfield Royal Canal Leisure Park was officially opened. The Enfield Group had completed all the work they had set out to do, including the installation of a new slipway which had been inaugurated in July of the previous year.

From 1986, the OPW itself became actively involved in the restoration of the canal. Most of its work was confined initially to dredging in the Dublin area: the ban on recruitment in the Public Service meant that staff could not be taken on to deal with the other sections. However, in 1987, Mr John McKeown was appointed as full-time engineer with special responsibility for the Royal Canal. Although restoration work on the canal was fragmented up to 1988 because of the involvement of both the OPW and of the different branches of the RCAG in their own areas, the different parts of the jig-saw had begun to fall into place by the end of that year. Although a considerable amount of restoration work was completed at this stage on the eastern section, the canal was still isolated from the rest of the inland waterway system. While there was water in the canal from the Liffey to Coolnahay, county Westmeath, it was only navigable in the county Kildare area from Confey near Leixlip to Maynooth Harbour. A considerable amount of dredging was still required on the Dublin section and on the section from Kilcock to Mullingar. New lock gates were also required on many of the locks. From Coolnahay to Richmond Harbour on the western section, only isolated shallow sections of water existed at Ballynacarrigy and at Abbeyshrule, county Longford.

Restoration 1988 *to* 1991

In 1988, the OPW began to supply timber to the RCAG to manufacture lock gates for the canal. It was hoped that by the end of December 1988 all of the gates required for the Dublin to Mullingar section would be completed. In the Dublin area, all the canal was in water although lock gates were required at the 7th, 8th and 9th locks. Many of the lock chambers on this section were filled with rubbish. The 1st lock at Charleville Mall off North Strand Road was choked with debris and it was estimated that there was up to four feet of silt in the lock chamber. Gaining access to clear this section would be difficult as the existing towpath would be unable to take the weight of a land dredger. Similarly at the 6th and 7th locks, the accumulation of rubbish from some nearby factories was a serious problem.

Installation by the OPW of the remaining lock gates on the eastern section of the canal began in December 1988. At the same time, all the levels on the Killucan flight were dredged (18th to 24th) and the surrounding area landscaped. In an effort to complete the navigation to Mullingar by October 1989 and to celebrate the bi-centenary of the signing of the Charter, the OPW provided a full time installation crew on the canal from

Figure 26: Lockhouse at the 1st lock, North Strand Road, Dublin

January 1989. A second crew was expected to be appointed by the end of March 1990.

No effort was spared by the OPW and by June 1989 gates were installed at the 16th, 18th, 19th, 21st and 22nd locks and installation work had begun on the 14th and 15th locks. By September 1989, the 14th, 15th and 17th locks were completed as well as the 23rd and 24th locks. Dredging continued on many stretches and the OPW transferred the 33M waterborne dredger from the Grand Canal to the Royal in order to dredge those sections that were inaccessible to the land dredger.

On Friday 5 January 1990 the lock gate factory at Watling Street closed. During the ten years of its existence, it had manufactured most of the gates required to complete the restoration between Dublin and Mullingar. The lock gate factory was undoubtedly the most important project undertaken by the RCAG for without it, no restoration could have taken place. By June 1990, the Royal Canal was completely restored to navigation between Blanchardstown, county Dublin and Mullingar, county Westmeath. To celebrate this event, the RCAG organised a week-long boat rally which stopped at all the restored harbours on the route. These were the first boats to reach Mullingar by the Royal Canal in thirty-five years.

Chapter Seven

The Future of the Royal Canal

The Canals Act 1986 finally transferred the ownership of the Grand and Royal Canals and the Barrow Navigation from Coras Iompair Éireann (CIE) to the Office of Public Works (OPW) in 1978. The purpose of the new Act was to secure the future of the waterways to which it related as a public amenity.[1]

In July 1986 at a ceremony in Tullamore, county Offaly, both the Grand and Royal Canals were officially vested in the OPW under the Act. The kernel of this Act is contained in Sections Five and Six which set out the general duties and powers of the Commissioners of the OPW. Their central function is to "undertake the care, management and maintenance of the canals and other canal property as a public amenity".

In September 1985 before the official handing over of the canals, the OPW commissioned a study[2] of the Grand and Royal Canals and the Barrow Navigation. The purpose of the study was to assess the condition of the navigations at that time and to advise as to how the waterways might be best developed. The results of this study were presented in 1988. The recommendations of this study are now accepted as the official plan for the development of the three navigations.

On 23 February 1988 the OPW published the study. It was carried out by a series of surveys of the waterway network which were conducted on foot, by boat and from the air, the latter including the making of an aerial video. The survey covered the condition and current use of the system, the characteristics of the system including environment and adjacent land use and the recording of features, facilities and areas of scientific interest.

The developments proposed in the study of the Royal Canal are to be for general amenity, particularly for local use. In the long term, the objective is to restore the whole canal, provided it is technically feasible to do so and subject to the necessary resources being made available.

The canal is to be developed in two ways: first as a fully navigable canal capable of being used primarily by cruisers and also by small boats, which could use the Royal Canal as part of the Irish inland waterway system; and secondly at various unspecified locations for amenity uses such as fishing, walking, canoeing, and the observation of vegetation and wild life.

It is acknowledged that the towns and villages along the canal are generally the major access points to the canal and mark the points of intersection between the canal and the road system. Therefore they are crucial to the development of the canal for they represent the locations at which most future land-based canal related development is likely to take place.

In the future it is hoped that in a number of towns and villages along the route either major or minor boat centres would be developed as well as overnight stops. Services provided at major boat centres would include long-term mooring, shops, toilets and public telephones. Other facilities would include fuel and water supply, refuse disposal and boat repair workshops.

Minor boat centres would cater for ten to thirty boats. Water, toilet and refuse disposal would be provided but repair service and refuelling facilities would not be available. It is proposed that such centres be located at Maynooth, Thomastown, Ballinea, Abbeyshrule and Longford.

Fishing

Fishing on the canal has increased in recent years. Stocking of the canal with fish is carried out, at present, by the Central Fisheries Board who are co-ordinating a research programme on the canal, funded by the OPW.[3] In the Dublin city and county areas, coarse fishing has developed well because of the canal's close proximity to large population centres such as Cabra, Finglas, Blanchardstown and Clonsilla. Fishing clubs have developed in some rural areas such as at Kilcock and Enfield and competitions are organised frequently on the long level. Some of these clubs also stock the canal with fish.

Fishing throughout the canal varies considerably. This is primarily due to changing depths and varying amounts of weed growth. In the Dublin area, roach and pike are plentiful. In the Enfield area, the canal is well stocked with small rudd, while the long level is the best stretch for bream and tench.[4] The Central Fisheries Board is responsible for overall policy with regard to fishing on the canals including the Barrow Navigation, while the Regional Fisheries Boards deal with the day-to-day development and operation of fishing in their specific areas.[5]

In the future it is hoped that a Fisheries Development Plan be drawn up for the Royal Canal and that, as part of this plan, a single body will manage and develop fishing on all the canals owned by the OPW.

Canal towpaths provide an excellent location for walking, especially in areas where there is an attractive canal environment. They also provide a potential location for a wide range of other informal activities such as nature study, picnicing and photography. These areas are also of value for those interested in the study of industrial archaeology.

In order to encourage some of the more informal activities described above, a guide was published in 1984 which outlines the route from Dublin to Richmond Harbour as well as historical and other items of interest along the way.[6] Walks along the Royal Canal are organised by An Óige and in the summer, guided walks and talks are organised by the RCAG. The presence of varied habitats and wildlife is considered one of the greatest attractions of the canal.

In order to encourage more people to avail of the canal for amenity use, the Development Study suggested that signposting, visitor information boards, and interpretative facilities should be introduced.[7] It is felt that this would ensure that the special qualities of the canal are more widely recognised and protected. The western section of the Royal Canal is considered to be a particularly important area for the development of walking as it provides potential links with existing walks in county Roscommon and from there to the Western Way.

Since the construction of the canals, a series of semi-natural habitats have developed along their length. Because of more intensive agriculture and increased urbanisation, the importance of such ecosystems has grown. In the case of Ireland, the opening of the canals allowed many Shannon and central plain lake species to spread eastwards.[8] At first, only the lightest and most mobile species were dispersed, carried by the flow of water and by the dragging action of the barges. The more heavily fruited species spread less quickly; for example, the yellow water-lily which spread from the river Shannon did not become common in the Dublin area until the early twentieth century. It is now found throughout the length of the Royal Canal.

Canals are ideally suited to abundant aquatic plant development.[9] Water flow is minimal and presents few problems for plant establishment. The relatively shallow depth of water allows submerged plants to grow across the full channel width and organically-rich mud deposits, resulting largely from aquatic plant degeneration, accumulate on the bed of the canal and provide a nutrient-rich substrate in which root plants can proliferate.

The foregoing features mean that canals provide areas of scientific interest to botanists and ecologists and a valuable educational resource. The Development Study suggested that this aspect was worthy of special care and consideration and it was recommended that any pressure to turn the Royal into manicured linear parks should be resisted in favour of a more natural presentation.

The potential value of canals as an ecological resource has been recognised by An Foras Forbartha[10] whose *Areas of Scientific Interest in Ireland* lists ten such areas on the Royal Canal alone. These areas will now be closely monitored by both the OPW and by the various local authorities through whose areas the canal passes. One type of area seen as requiring particular attention was the raised peat bogs. These are now recognised as rare habitats in a European context and their management and protection is thus a matter for concern. It is envisaged that by the end of the century many of the bogs which adjoin the Royal Canal will have been cut away due to harvesting. It is hoped that liaison will take place with Bord na Móna with a view to pressing for the retention of the remaining undisturbed bogs.

At the outset, the Royal Canal project might have seemed to be an overly optimistic enterprise. Certainly, the initial incompetence of the company and its directors suggested that the project might never be completed to the river Shannon. Upon its completion, the canal never generated the expected levels of traffic and was a loss-maker. Closure was inevitable. Yet, the future is now bright and, two hundred years on, the canal may be about to generate significant benefits which were undreamt of by John Binns and his fellow promoters.

References

CHAPTER ONE

1 2 Geo. 1 c.12 (1715).
2 First Report of the Royal Commission appointed to inspect, enquire into and report on canals and inland navigation of the United Kingdom, 1906. Minutes of Evidence Appendix 2.
3 Commons Jr. Ire. 1715-30. III, Pt. I, p.331.
4 An Act to encourage tillage and better employment of the poor and also for better putting into effect the 1715 Act.
5 Ruth Delany. *A Celebration of 250 Years of Ireland's Inland Waterways*. (Belfast 1986.) p.190.
6 V. T. H. and D. R. Delany. *The Canals of the South of Ireland*. (David and Charles 1966) p. 19.
7 Commons Jr. Ire. 1749-56 8 October. V, p.224.
8 Ibid. 1 November 1755. p.230.
9 Ibid. 8 November 1755. p.241.
10 Ibid. 12 November 1755. p.245.
11 Ibid. 17 February 1755. p.368.
12 Ibid, p.370.
13 Ibid.
14 (Anon.) Mr. Omer's Letters to the Public Controller of Inland Navigation (Dublin 1755). (Anon.) Mr. Omer's letter to the public Controller examined, and the observations on the said letter observed upon. (Dublin 1755). (Anon.) A description of the River Lines for an Inland Navigation in Ireland from Dublin to the Shannon with some remarks upon them. Dublin 1756.
15 (Anon.) An Account of the Rise and Progress of the Royal Canal in Ireland and also of the Opposition thereto. (Dublin 1797).
16 Commons Jr. Ire. 1783-85 XI, Pt.1. p.453.
17 Ibid. Pt. II, App. CCLXXXVII, 7 February 1785.
18 29 Geo. III c.33 (1789).

CHAPTER TWO

1 Canals and Waterways Commission 1923. Minutes of Evidence, Nineteenth Day 6 March. p.1.
2 L.M. Cullen, *An Economic History of Ireland Since 1660* (London 1972), p.100

3 Commons Jr. Ire. 26 March 1788 Pt.1, XIII, p.120.
4 Samuel Smiles. *Lives of the Engineers.* Vol. II (London 1874), p.238.
5 *Wilson's Dublin Directory* (Dublin 1789) p.62.
6 Ibid. p.128
7 *Gentleman's and Citizens' Almanac* (Dublin 1789) p.96.
8 J. W. Hammond. Mr. William Cope's petition 1804. *Dublin Historical Record* Vol. VI 1933/34. p.25-38.
9 B.P.P. 1810-11 (235) VI, 33.
10 Commons Jr. Ire. 13 March 1789-90 XIII, p.5.
11 *Dublin Gazette* December 16-18 1788).
12 Commons Jr. Ire. 25 March 1788. XII, Pt.II, p.419.
13 The Charter of the Royal Canal Company October 1789.
14 Commons Jr. Ire. 13 March 1789-90 XIII, p.62.
15 Ibid. 16 March. App. CLXXI.
16 Ibid. 18 April. p.85-6.
17 Ibid. 18 April. p.77.
18 Ibid. 20 April. p.86.
19 Ibid. p.87
20 Report from Committee on Petition of Royal Canal Company 1811 B.P.P. 1810-11 (235) VI.28.
21 Commons Jr. Ire. 1796 XVI, App. DXXXIV-DXXXVI.
22 Ruth Delany, *The Grand Canal of Ireland* (David and Charles 1973) p.32.
23 Letter to the Royal Canal Company.1790.
24 Charles Vallancey, *A treatise on Inland Navigation or the Art of Making Rivers Navigable, of making Canals in all sorts of Soils and of Construction Locks and Sluices.* (Dublin 1763).
25 *Dublin Journal*, 21 April. 1796.
26 Commons Jr. Ire. 1792/4 XV, Pt. II App. DCLXIX-DCLXXI.
27 The only surviving example of these maps which is known to the author is: MS. Map of Intended Line for Royal Canal from the county of Dublin Boundary at St. Catherines to Kilcock as laid out by R. Evans, surveyed by John Brownrigg. At James Maxwell's House Maynooth. One Sheet Parchment 12'4" X 2'. September 1791. NLI.
28 *Freemans Journal* 19 October 1789.
29 Ibid. 14 November 1789.
30 Delany. *The Grand Canal.* op. cit. p.35.
31 Report of Committee appointed by Royal Canal Company. (Dublin 1793).
32 Delany. *The Grand Canal.* op. cit. p.35.
33 Royal Canal Report.1793 op. cit.
34 Commons Jr. Ire. 1792-94 XV, Pt.II, App. DCLXXIX.

35 Commons Jr. Ire. 26 February 1789/90 XIII, p.188.
36 Parliamentary Register (Dublin 1790) p.326.
37 A. A. Horner, The Development of Towns and Villages, county Kildare, in *A Geographical Background for Planning* 1970 (Dept. of Geography, T.C.D. 1970) pp.55-6.

CHAPTER THREE

1 The first report of work having commenced was in the *Freeman's Journal* 6th May 1790.
2 Commons Jr. Ire. 1794 Pt.II,XV, App. DCLCCCII-DCLXXXIII.
3 Ibid. 1791 XIV, App. CXXII.
4 The Address of Richard Evans, Engineer to the Royal Canal Company. (Dublin 1793)
5 Ibid.
6 Anthony Burton, *The Canal Builders* (London 1972). It was customary in the English canal system to appoint engineers in this way.
7 Commons Jr. Ire. 1791 XIV, p.426-7.
8 Ibid, p.429.
9 Commons Jr. Ire. 1794 Pt. II XV, App. DCLCIII.
10 Ibid. 1792 Pt. II, XV, App. DCX
11 Address of Richard Evans op.cit.
12 Commons Jr. Ire. 1796 XXI, App. DXXXIV-DXXX
13 Ibid. App. DXXXIV-DXXXVI.
14 Commons Jr. Ire. 1794 Pt. II, XV, App. DCXL-DCXLI
15 Ibid. App. DCXXXI
16 Royal Canal Committee Report 1793.
17 Ibid.
18 Brownrigg to Hatch 23 December 1795. (Hatch Papers 1795-9). NLI.
19 Commons Jr. Ire. 1794 Pt. II, XV, App. DCXXII
20 Royal Canal Committee Report 1793. op. cit. p.4.
21 Commons Jr. Ire. 1794 Pt. II, XV, App. DCXXXIII.
22 Ibid. p.335.
23 Ibid. 1796 XVI, App. DXXXIV-DXXXVI.
24 Ibid.
25 38 Geo. III c.79. (1798).
26 Commons Jr. Ire. 26 March 1788 Pt. I, XII, p.120.
27 Ibid. 1800 Pt. II, XIX, 23 June p.223. App. MVI
28 40 Geo. III c.51.(1800).
29 Minutes Book of the Directors General of Inland Navigation 25 August 1800-3 December 1801. Hereafter referred to as Minute Book. D.G.I.N.

30 Minute Book, D.G.I.N. 25 August 1800 to 3 December 1801.
31 Engineers Report Book, Directors General of Inland Navigation 7-9-1800 to 9-2-1802
32 Minutes Book D.G.I.N. 25 August 1800 - 3 December 1801.
33 Report from Committee on Petition of Royal Canal Company 1811. B.P.P. 1810-11 (235) VI, 28
34 Report from Committee appointed to enquire into tolls on the Royal Canal 1805.B.P.P.1805 (169) IV.484.
35 Report from Committee on Petition of Royal Canal Company B.P.P. 1810-11 (235) VI, 41.
36 Minute Book D.G.I.N. 17 July 1807 - 21 June 1808.
37 Report from Committee on Inland Navigation Ireland. B.P.P. 1812-13 (198) VI.20-23.
38 Minute Book D.G.I.N. 21-6-1806 to 17-7-1807.
39 Report of the Directors General upon the affairs of the Royal Canal Company B.P.P. 1810-11 (190) VI.48-9.
40 B.P.P. 1812-13 (198) VI, 35.
41 55 Geo. III C 182.(1815)
42 Second Report of a Committee appointed to enquire into and examine the claims of the Royal Canal Company and other matters relating to said Company. 1815. B.P.P. 1814-15 (453), VI, 1759.
43 58 Geo. III c.35. (1818)
44 Letter Books Royal Canal Board of Control 6 October 1818
45 Report of Committee on Inland Navigation. To take into consideration the state of the Grand and Royal Canal Companies and the state of inland navigation. B.P.P. 1812/13 (198) VI, 21-4
46 Minute Book D.G.I.N. 24 February 1813 - 8 March 1814.
47 Ibid.
48 Ibid.
49 Samuel Draper, Royal Canal Company Secretary to Robert Peel 10 November 1812 (Papers Relating to Inland Navigation in Ireland). Copies of Correspondence between His Majesty's Government and the Royal Canal Company and other papers; relative to the state of their affairs from 29 November 1812-15 February 1813.
50 Minute Book. D.G.I.N. 24 February 1813-19 October 1814.
51 Ibid.
52 Ibid.
53 Inland Waterways Commission 1923, Minutes of Evidence, 5 March 1923. p.4.
54 Ibid.

55 Minute Book of the New Royal Canal Company 26 August 1822 hereafter referred to as Minute Book Royal Canal Company
56 Report of a Committee of Proprietors of the New Royal Canal Company inculpatory of the Management of the Board of Directors of that Concern with replies... vindicatory of the Board's Management (Dublin 1834).p.29. Hereafter referred to as Report of Proprietors of New Royal Canal Company
57 Royal Canal Minutes 22 November 1823.
58 *Dublin Gazette* 16 June 1827
59 Royal Canal Minutes January 1830.

CHAPTER FOUR

1 A. McCutcheon, *The Transport Revolution, Canals and River Navigations, in Travel and Transport in Ireland*, pp 64-81 Ed. Kevin B. Nowlan (Dublin 1973).
2 *Walker's Hibernian Magazine*, December 1796. p.266.
3 J. C. McCraken. *Travel and Transport 1973.* op. cit. pp.47-63.
4 *The Gentleman's and Citizens' Almanac* (Dublin 1797) p.113-5.
5 Report from Committee on Petition of Royal Canal Company, 1811, B.P.P. 1810-11 (235), VI, 41.
6 Commons Jr. Ire. 1800. XII Pt. II App. MXXI-MXXIII.
7 Horner op.cit. p.61
8 *Dublin Chronicle* December 1791
9 Thomas Cromwell, *Excursions through Ireland* (Essex 1820) p.157.
10 Constantia Maxwell. *The Stranger in Ireland* (London 1954) p.233.
11 Delany. *Canals of the South of Ireland*, op. cit. p.193.
12 Petition of Royal Canal Company. 1811. B.P.P. 1810-11 (235), VI, 41.
13 Ibid. 31.
14 *The Gentleman's and Citizens' Almanac* (Dublin 1806) p.122.
15 Ibid. (Dublin 1807) p.126-7
16 Petition of Royal Canal Company. 1811. B.P.P. 1810-11 (235), VI, 41.
17 Papers Relating to Inland Navigation; 1813. B.P.P. 1812-13 (61), VI, 317, App. 10.B.
18 Minute Book D.G.I.N. 14-2-1812 - 12-22-2 1813.

19 Delany. *The Grand Canal.* op. cit. p.107
20 Delany. *Canals of the South of Ireland.* op. cit. p.206.
21 Minute Book Royal Canal Company, 31 March 1819.
22 Ibid. 25 June 1819.
23 Ibid. 28 October 1819.
24 Ibid. 17 April 1919.
25 Ibid. 21 October 1819.
26 *Freeman's Journal,* June 1790.
27 *Dublin Evening Post,* October 10, 1807.
28 Minute Book Royal Canal Company March 1819.
29 O.P. 388/10.
30 Minute Book Royal Canal Company. June 1819.
31 Ibid. April 1821.
32 Ibid. October 1825
33 Ibid. 5 April 1832.
34 Ruth Delany. *Canaliana* Vol.8 1975. pp. 20-5.
35 Minute Book Royal Canal Company 22 April 1822.
36 Report on the half yearly accounts 30 September 1825 in Minute Book Royal Canal Company September 1825.
37 Ibid. 30 September 1823 Minute Book Royal Canal Company 2 July 1823.
38 Ibid. 2 July 1832.
39 Report of Proprietors of the New Royal Canal Company
40 Minute Book Royal Canal Company July 1832.
41 Alex Gordon, *Treastise upon Elemental Locomotion and Interior Communications,* (London 1834).
42 Minute Book Royal Canal Company July 1833.
43 Mr. & Mrs. S. C. Hall, *Ireland its Scenery and Character* (London 1841-43) Vol. III, p.275.
44 Second Report of the Commissioners Appointed to Consider and Recommend a General System of Railways for Ireland. B.P.P. 1837-8, XXXV, App. B, No. 6.
45 Canal Traffic Act. 1888. The Royal Canal. Proceedings Before the Hononary T. H. Pelham April 1894.
46 *Thom's Directory* 1850.
47 Ibid. 1847
48 Ibid. 1848.
49 Cullen. *Economic History of Ireland.* op. cit. p.104.
50 Joseph Lee. The Railway in the Irish Economy in *The Formation of Irish Economy* Ed. by L. M. Cullen (Cork 1969) p.78.
51 Arthur Young. *A Tour of Ireland* 1776-79. Ed. A. M. Hutton (London 1892) Vol. II p.81.
52 Robert Thomson. *Statistical Survey of county Meath.* (Dublin 1802) p.370.
53 *Freeman's Journal* 10 December 1801.

54 Cullen. *Economic History of Ireland.* op. cit. p.89.
55 A. A. Horner. Development of Towns West of Dublin. Ph.D. thesis. (T.C.D.) 1968.
56 Commons Jr. Ire. 1800 XII Pt. II. App. MXXI-MXXIII.
57 Ibid. 1798 XVII Pt. II. App. CCCCXXV.
58 Report of John Brownrigg on the Royal Canal for Directors General of Inland Navigation 1801.Engineers Report Book. D.G.I.N.
59 Commons Jr. Ire. 1800 XII Pt. II. App. MXXI-MXXIII.
60 Cullen, *An Economic History of Ireland.* op. cit. p.100.
61 Minute Book D.G.I.N. 25 August 1800-3 December 1801 p.110.
62 Engineers Report Book, D.G.I.N. 29 December 1808.
63 E. B. McGuire. *Irish Whiskey. A History of Distilling, the Spirit Trade and Excise Controls in Ireland.* (Dublin 1973)
64 Commons Jr. Ire. 1800 XII Pt.2. App. MXXI-MXXIII.
65 Minute Book Royal Canal Company 20 October 1818.
66 Ibid.
67 Ibid. 6 October 1818.
68 Ibid. 13 October 1821
69 Ibid. 8 March 1821.
70 Ibid. 4 July 1822.
71 Cullen, *Economic History of Ireland.* op. cit. p.109.
72 Minute Book Royal Canal Company 4 September 1820.
73 Ibid. 25 February 1822.
74 Minute Book Royal Canal Company 12 August 1822.
75 Royal Canal Rental Ledger 1818/46 900 year lease to Thomas Bryan from 1 May 1822 at £9 ground rent per annum.
76 Minute Book Royal Canal Company 1822.
77 Ibid.
78 Ibid. April 1825.
79 Ibid. July 1825.
80 Ibid. August 1825.
81 Ibid. 28 October 1822.
82 Ibid. 4 November 1822.
83 Ibid. 29 April 1822.
84 John Cooke, Bog Reclamation, Peat Development in county Kildare. *Journal of County Kildare Archaeological Society.* No. 5 (1970).
85 Minute Book Royal Canal Company January 1822.
86 Ibid. 15 October 1822.
87 Ibid. August 1824.
88 Ibid. November 1824.
89 Robert Kane, *The Industrial Resources of Ireland* (Dublin 1845) pp.40-42.

90 Cullen. *Economic History of Ireland.* op. cit. p.104.
91 Minute Book Royal Canal Company February 1820.
92 Ibid. February 1820.
93 Ibid. April 1824.
94 Ibid.
95 Summary Digest of Evidence taken before The Select Committee of the House of Lords, on the State of Ireland in Respect to Crime, as Relating to the Ribbon Society (Dublin 1839).
96 Minute Book Royal Canal Company January 1823.
97 Ibid. Report of half yearly account for 31 March 1825.
98 Delany. *Ireland's Inland Waterways.* op. cit. p.60.

CHAPTER FIVE

1 Report from Select Committee on Industries (Ireland) B.P.P.1884-5 (288) IXI 94-575
2 Board of Control Letter Books 4 December 1845
3 9 and 10 VIC. c.210 (1846).
4 *Canals and Inland Waterways Commission* Minutes of Evidence Nineteenth Day 6 March 1923. p.19
5 Ibid.
6 *Railway and Canal Traffic Act 1888.* Royal Canal Minutes of Evidence Tatlow. para. 2426-24267.
7 S. Maxwell Hajducki *A Railway Atlas of Ireland*, (David and Charles) (1974)
8 Royal Canal Trade Ledger 1952-54.
9 Number of pigs brought by Royal Canal to Dublin. B.P.P.1834 (532) XVII. 223
10 Cullen, *Economic History of Ireland*, op. cit. p.137
11 Second Report of the Commissioners appointed to inspect the accounts and examine the works of railways in Ireland B.P.P.1868-9. XXXII, App. IV.
12 *Waterways Commission 1923.* Minutes of Evidence Nineteenth Day. p.13.
13 Ibid.
14 *The Irish Builder.* Vol. XXI. February 1879. p.62
15 *Waterways Commission 1923.* Minutes of Evidence Nineteenth Day.
16 *Railway and Canal Traffic Act 1888.*
17 Ibid.
18 *Dublin Gazette* 25 June 1879.
19 *Waterways Commission 1923* Minutes of Evidence Nineteenth Day p.5

20 *Railway and Canal Traffic Act 1888*. Royal Canal Minutes of Evidence. Merodith para. 1933-4.
21 Poster of tolls, wharfage etc. and also rates of freight chargeable on the Royal Canal 1856.
22 *Railway and Canal Traffic Act 1888*. Royal Canal Minutes of Evidence Kennedy para. 24811-24815.
23 Ibid. Williams para. 24449-24450.
24 *Royal Commission on Canals and Waterways 1906*. Evidence of George Stevens 6 October 1906. B.P.P. 1909 (XXXIII) Pt.I.
25 *Railway and Canal Traffic Act 1888*. Royal Canal Minutes of Evidence. Mooney. para. 24558-24581
26 Ibid.
27 Edward Patterson. *History of the Londonderry and Lough Swilly Railway*. (David and Charles 1964) p.32.
28 *Royal Commission 1906* Stevens *op.cit.* 1906.B.P.P. 1909. (XXXIII) Pt. I
29 Ibid.
30 Ibid.
31 *Irish Builder*, Vol. XXXVII 15 August 1895. p.15.
32 *Waterways Commission 1923*. Twenty-first Day. p.4.
33 Ibid.
34 *Royal Commission* 1906 B.P.P. (II). Pt. II. App. 20
35 Ibid. B.P.P. 1911 (XIII) App.19 p.39.
36 *Royal Commission* 1906. B.P.P. 1909 (XXXIII) App. 1. Statement 2.
37 Ibid.
38 *Waterways Commission 1923* Twenty-First Day p.9.
39 57 and 58 VIC.(1894).
40 *Waterways Commission* Nineteenth Day p.53.
41 Ibid. Twenty-First Day p.14
42 Ibid. Twentieth Day p.44.
43 Ibid. p.39.
44 Ibid. p.44.
45 Ibid. Twenty-first Day.
46 Ibid.
47 Ibid. Twentieth Day.
48 Ibid. Nineteenth Day p.11.
49 These details were established with Mr. Michael Mallin of Kilcock, who worked as a boatman on the Royal Canal from a very early age until his retirement in 1951. Mr. Mallin's father and grandfather were also boatmen
50 Gerard Quinn and Patrick Lynch. *The Latest Phase in Irish Transport*. Nawlon *op.cit.* p.150
51 Ibid.
52 L.T.C. Rolt. *Green and Silver* (London 1946) pp.108-28.

53 An Act to enable CIE to close the Royal Canal to navigation and to provide for matters related to such a closure (21 December 1960)

CHAPTER SIX

1 Delany. *Ireland's Inland Waterways.* op. cit. p.177.
2 A. J. McEvoy. The Royal Canal Resurgence *Canaliana* 1972. p.22.
3 *Inland Waterways News.* March 1974
4 *The Royal Canal as an Amenity.* A proposed scheme for preservation and restoration (Inland Waterways Association of Ireland 1974).
5 *Royal Canal News* Issue No. 1. 1974.
6 Ibid. Issue No. 2. January 1975
7 Ibid. Issue No. 3. Summer 1975.
8 *Transportation in Dublin* p.22. (An Foras Fortartha 1971).
9 *Dublin Development Plan* 1971 Map 2.
10 *Dublin Development Plan Policy-Trends* Para. 2:39 pp. 17-40.
11 Draft Development Plan Review 1976. Map 1.
12 *Future of the Grand and Royal Canal* issued by Government Information Service on behalf of the Department of Tourism and Transport. 30 November 1978.
13 *Restoration of the Royal Canal a detailed Plan.* Inland Waterways Association of Ireland. 1979.
14 *R.C. News.* Issue No. 13 April 1980.
The details for the rest of this chapter are taken from *R.C. News* 1980 to 1991. (Supplied by Mr Fergus Flanagan).

CHAPTER SEVEN

1 An Act to make provision for the transfer of the Grand Canal and Royal Canal from CIE to the Commissioners of Public Works in Ireland and to provide for other matters connected therewith. (11 March 1986).
2 *Grand Canal, Royal Canal, Barrow Navigation Management Development Strategy.* Prepared for the Office of Public Works by Brady, Shipman, Martin 1987.
3 Dr. Joseph Caffrey. Fish Research on the Royal Canal at Kilcock. *R.C. News.* Issue 31 December 1988.

4 Hugh Gough, Coarse Angling Officer, Central Fisheries Board. Fishing on the Royal Canal in Ruth Delany and Ian Bath *Guide to the Royal Canal of Ireland* (Dublin 1984).
5 *Development Study* 1987 Section 6. p.54.
6 Delany and Bath. *op.cit.*
7 *Development Study* 1987. op. cit. p.56.
8 Declan Doogue. The Spread of the Canal Flora. *Canaliana* Vol. 8. 1975. p.40.
9 Dr. Joseph Caffrey. Weed Management in Irish Canals. *R.C.News* Issue 38 September/December 1990.
10 *Areas of Scientific Interest in Ireland.* An Foras Forbartha (Dublin 1981).

Appendix A

Tonnage of Goods Carried on the Royal Canal

Tonnage of Goods Carried
on Royal Canal from 1836-1838

Goods	1836 Tons	1837 Tons	1838 Tons
Live Pigs	36,002	34,349	15,669
Casks Butter	7,639	3,638	3,812
Corn/Meal			
Potatoes	31,746	26,024	15,881
General Merchandise	7,355	6,247	3,373
Coal/Manure	14,344	14,559	4,145
Stone/Bricks	11,894	16,127	6,414
Turf	22,992	21,724	10,214
Total Tonnage for Year	131,972	122,668	59,508

Total tonnage carried
1836 to 1838 = 314,148

Tonnage of Goods Carried on Royal Canal from 1807-1811

Type of Merchandise	1807 Tons	1807 £-s-d	1808 Tons	1808 £-s-d	1809 Tons	1809 £-s-d	1810 Tons	1810 £-s-d	1811 Tons	1811 £-s-d	Total Tons Over 5 Years
General Merchandise	4,580.85	1,315-10-02	4,083.00	1,246-12-11	5,795.15	1,633-07-07	5,128.80	1,324-04-09	5,166.85	1,579-12-04	24,754.65
Flour	60.65	8-01-00	174.55	15-06-00	382.90	41-16-02	318.00	44-07-02	805.05	105-13-07	1,741.15
Grain	2,954.30	365-06-11	4,922.80	651-10-05	5,620.85	776-19-02	5,699.00	859-00-01	9,236.05	1,414-19-06	28,433.00
Meal	36.10	3-02-04	53.60	6-16-10	264.95	39-12-09	273.05	40-06-06	183.65	24-06-05	811.35
Malt	129.50	20-01-03	35.15	4-19-05	9.00	2-11-00	35-30	6-11-05	3.00	10-03	211.95
Potatoes	780.30	36-09-01	852.70	47-07-11	2,813.90	202-13-06	8,899.35	724-18-08	6,953.10	536-01-00	20,299.40
Dung	2,278.80	83-03-03	3,201.50	114-13-11	3,760.90	111-06-04	3,312.65	86-09-02	5,171.40	110-12-09	17,725.25
Turf	1,533.75	77-05-07	1,583.10	78-19-00	2,633.70	221-00-05	4,184.40	370-13-07	3,585.05	355-00-07	13,520.00
Timber	665.85	157-10-00	428.10	94-18-03	878.50	172-09-04	923.20	169-01-09	734.10	186-06-03	3,629.75
Coal	2,841.70	188-08-03	5,687.50	520-16-09	3,359.15	281-05-09	4,854.35	384-09-02	5,776.90	507-01-11	22,519.60
Bricks	7,731.00	413-09-11	5,929.10	285-16-11	3,696.65	231-01-00	5,108.10	342-04-08	11,621.90	539-01-00	34,086.75
Limestone	2,628.95	140-05-08	11,071.90	511-07-06	3,473.90	155-17-00	4,620.95	179-19-02	6,052.05	329-06-06	27,847.75
Stone Flags	8,357.70	477-00-01	8,689.35	375-16-11	13,101.75	621-13-04	6,168.05	343-16-08	5,381.75	255-14-10	41,698.60
Sand/Gravel	1,212.20	54-03-09	2,582.70	130-05-07	806.80	34-11-09	2,405.75	72-02-01	3,257.90	151-12-03	10,265.35
Iron	577.20	63-01-11	980.65	108-06-03	863.80	102-08-03	677.50	73-16-02	1,057.95	124-08-08	4,157.10
Hay/Straw	26.75	1-05-02	178.65	8-18-00	73.95	5-10-11	20.05	1-19-09	60.60	5-13-05	360.00
Lime					73.65	3-03-11					73.65
Military					68.00	1-01-10					68.00
Totals	36,395.65	£3,406-06-07	50,454.35	£4,202-03-00	47,677.50	£4,638-00-03	52,628.50	£5,025-02-11	65,047.30	£6,230-03-06	252,203.30

Tonnage of Goods Carried on Royal Canal from 1839 to 1845

Goods OUTWARDS	1839 Tons	1840 Tons	1841 Tons	1842 Tons	1843 Tons	1844 Tons	1845 Tons
Coal/Manure	16,278.00	17,176.45	19,471.05	17,707.25	13,719.25	13,184.80	14,884.90
General Merchandise	8,857.10	8,863.05	9,067.20	9,775.20	8,362.70	10,164.10	11,157.40
Sub Total	25,135.10	26,039.50	28,538.25	27,482.45	22,081.95	23,348.90	26,042.30
INWARDS							
Stone/Sand Flags/Bricks	13,482.45	16,056.15	16,240.18	12,771.75	19,563.85	23,110.70	18,168.45
Turf	20,645.95	10,635.95	14,428.14	11,785.10	11,518.85	10,904.15	12,326.70
Corn/Meal Potatoes/Butter Live Pigs	23,725.45	24,939.30	25,650.10	21,654.10	30,036.55	33,702.10	31,604.60
Sub Total	57,853.85	51,631.40	56,318.42	46,210.95	61,119.25	67,716.95	62,099.75
Total Tonnage Per Year	82,988.95	77,670.90	84,856.67	73,693.40	83,201.20	91,065.85	88,142.05
Total Yearly Tolls		£11,505-7-4	£10,687-6-1	£11,469-19-8	£11,665-15-8	£13,357-19-6	£13,737-16-9

Tonnage of Goods Carried on the Royal Canal from 1846-1851

Goods OUTWARDS	1846 Tons	1847 Tons	1848 Tons	1849 Tons	1850 Tons	1851 Tons
Coal/Manure	12,222.00	11,065.35	14,343.90	14,005.50	14,942.95	11,063.80
General Merchandise	16,749.10	42,377.65	35.309.40	34,722.60	21,692.50	39,921.65
Sub Total	28,971.10	53,443.00	49,653.30	48,728.10	36,635.45	50,985.45
INWARDS	Tons	Tons	Tons	Tons	Tons	Tons
Stone/Sand Flags/Bricks	29,828.35	38,190.05	32,107.45	28,016.80	23,254.20	24,788.85
Turf	11,221.50	10,708.10	10,242.70	8,510.70	9,632.40	9,171.55
Corn/Meal Potatoes/Butter Live Pigs	29,799.25	9,839.90	17,798.75	15,882.50	24,156.00	16,370.05
Sub Total	70,849.10	58,738.05	60,148.90	52,410.00	57,042.60	50,330.45
Total Tonnage per Year	99,820.20	112,181.05	109,802.20	101,138.10	93,678.05	101,315.90
Total Yearly Tolls	£12,474-4-6	£13,931-18-4	£13,578-12-6	£12,568-19-1	£10,760-4-8	£13,357-19-6

Appendix B

List of Subscribers of the Royal Canal Company 1789

£	
1,000	His Grace the Duke of Leinster
1,000	Right Hon. the Earl of Granard
1,000	Right Hon. the Lord Longford
600	Right Hon. Earl Carhampton
1,000	Right Hon. Lord Sunderlin
600	Right Hon. Viscount Ranelagh
1,000	Right Hon. Lord Trimelston
600	Hon. Lord Devlin
600	Right Hon. Sir John Blacquiere K.B.
1,000	Right Hon. Thomas Connolly
1,800	Sir William Gleadowe Newcomen Bart.
1,000	Sir Thomas Fetherston Bart.
600	Sir Robert Hodson Bart.
600	Hon. Robert Rochford
1,200	Hon. Richard Annesley
600	Hon. Capt. Thomas Pakenham
600	Robert Alexander
600	Arthur Dawson
1,000	John Hatch
1,000	Henry Cope
2,000	William Cope
2,000	John Binns
2,000	George Digby
2,000	Henry Stevens Riely
2,000	Randall McDonnell
3,000	John Jones
2,000	John Giffard
2,000	William Sinnett
2,000	Michael Allen
2,000	James Napper Tandy
2,000	Charles Clarke
2,000	William Pike
2,000	Thomas Tweedy
2,000	William Crosby

1,000	Pat McLoughlin
1,000	John Copeland
1,000	Arthur Riky
1,000	Christopher Deey
1,000	James Connolly
1,000	Mrs Ann Reilly
1,000	Alexander Kirkpatrick
1,000	William Huttenville
1,000	Thomas Andrews
1,000	Mrs Jane Hardin
1,000	Edward Bulkely
1,000	Capt. John Pratt
1,000	John Williams
1,000	Thomas Mangan
1,000	Peter Hoey
1,000	Edward Clarke
1,000	Nicholas Tallon
1,000	Solomon Boileau
1,000	Richard Allen
1,000	Robert Deey
1,000	William Shannon
1,000	William Taylor
1,000	James Fleming
1,000	Charles Ward
1,000	Charles Dillon Bellew
1,000	Thomas Dillon
1,000	Richard Whitten
1,000	Richard Cudmore
1,000	Daniel Finn
1,000	John Busby
1,000	Henry Strong
1,000	Major Joseph Walker
1,000	Timothy Dyton
1,000	Thomas Walker
1,000	John Collins
900	George Binns
700	Mrs Elizabeth Archibold
600	Sir John Nugent Bart.
600	Sir Charles Levinge Bart.
600	Thomas Tenison
600	Galper Erck
600	Capt. William Wright

600 Andrew Gibbons
600 John Crosthwaite
600 John Talbot
600 Brent Neville
600 John Allen
600 William Twigg
600 Sir Henry Jebb Kt.
600 Rev. George Coates
600 Charles Hamilton
600 John Keogh
600 Samuel Stock
600 Rev. Meade Dennis
600 William Norris
600 Charles Ryan
600 Thomas Darcy
600 Thomas Lynch
600 James Faucett
600 Daniel Reily
600 Henry Arabin
600 Mrs Mary Reily
600 George Clibborn
600 Andrew Higginbottom
600 Benjamin Clarke
600 William Featherston
600 Ralph Mulhern
600 Mark Anthony Blair
600 Henry Hutton
600 John Chambers
600 Joshua Dixon
600 Robert Joseph Shutter
600 Rev. Henry Wynne
600 John Reily
600 John Tyrell
600 Arthur Tyrell
600 James Henry
600 Henry Jackson
600 Andrew Daly MD
600 Francis Hopkins
600 Charles Thorp
600 Valentine Dillon
600 William Clarke
600 James Dixon

600 Robert Percival MD
600 James Kelly
600 Thomas Barrows
500 Miss Mary Thewless
500 James Middleton Berry
500 Samuel Downes
500 Mrs Mary Connor
500 John Ludeveze
500 John Verschoyle
500 John Barber
500 Joseph Donnelly
400 Whitmore Davis
300 Alderman Henry Grove Shankey
300 Alderman William Alexander
300 Alexander Lynar
300 Nathaniel Cartland
300 Charles Crosthwaite
300 Capt. Richard Chevenix
300 Reily Birminham
300 John Sankey
300 Hartley Hodson
300 Joseph Hubard
300 Ross Maguire
300 John White
300 Jasper Debrisay
300 James Ormsby
300 John Reynell
300 Nicholas Le Favre
300 Alexander Burrowes
300 Thomas Hackett
300 Philip Thomas Morpie
300 Alexander Lindsay MD
300 Capt. John Daniel Arabin
300 Gerald O'Ferral
300 James Carey
300 William Judge
300 Robert Walsh
300 John Johnston
300 John O'Brien
300 Michael Doyle
300 John Carey
300 Messdames C. and E. Fitzpatrick

300	John Ward
300	Samuel Ward
300	Andrew Clark
300	Walter Rooney
300	Terence Duff
300	Richard Fagan
300	Mathias Flood
300	James O'Brien
300	Robert Farrell
300	John Smith
300	Christopher Carey
300	Charles O'Connor
300	Myles Keon
300	Peter Delamere
300	Thomas Hickey
300	Bryan Kerin
300	William Russel
300	Henry Frazer
300	John Ferral
300	Patrick Byrne
300	James Crosby
300	Messrs. James Farrell and William Davett
300	Arthur Brown Governor Kinsale & c
300	Patrick Corcoran
100	Miss Letitia Vesey
100	Nathaniel Low
100	Thomas Shutter
100	John Alder

Although Francis Fetherston is named as a Royal Canal undertaker, he is not listed as a subscriber.

The Company's subscriptions and their financial transactions during the period of construction were carried out in Irish Currency.

The conversion rate was as follows:

£ 300 Irish = 276-18-5½ British
£1,000 Irish = 923- 1-6½ British
£2,000 Irish = 1846- 3-1 British

Appendix C

Boat Owners operating on the Royal Canal 1826 to 1847

1	Bagwell (bought from Flood 1844)
2	Behan
2	Blanchford
1	Branagan
1	Brennan
2	Brey
1	Bryan
1	Butler
3	Byrne
1	Cahill (bought from Kennedy 1843)
1	Casey
3	Carey
2	Carroll
3	Coffey
2	Commins
1	Conell
1	Cooke
2	Corcoran
3	Corey
1	Coyle
1	Coyne (bought from Fitzsimmons 1849)
3	Cribben
1	Dargan
1	Doran
1	Doyle
1	Dowling
12	Duffy Bros.
8	Dunne
1	Dwyer
1	Farr
1	Fitzgerald
1	Fitzsimmons
1	Fleming
1	Flood
1	Fox

2 Fullan
2 Gahagan
1 Gill
1 Glynn
1 Goodwin
1 Gorman
1 Green
1 Hanlon
3 Healy
1 Hyden
6 Kelly
1 Killmurray
1 Lawless
2 Leonard
1 Lynch
5 McCann
1 McCormick (bought from Edge 1845)
1 McGuire
4 Midland Great Western Railway
1 Maher
1 Moore
1 Morgan
5 Murphy
6 Murtagh
3 Nesbit
2 Odlum
1 Peppard
9 Pilsworth
1 Rooney
4 Royal Canal Company
1 Ryan
3 Shaw
1 Singleton
1 Slevin
2 Stenson
1 Tanard
1 Themson
2 Walsh
3 Ward
1 Wheatley
1 White
4 Williamson
1 Wilson

Appendix D

Accounts of the Royal Canal Company 1790-1810

	The Company's Stock £	Dividend per cent	Total Dividend £	Annual Debt. £	Permanent Expenditure £-s-d	Temporary Expenditure £-s-d	Permanent Revenue £-s-d
1790	200,000	No Dividend			- -	15,383- 2- 7	- -
1791		D°			- -	36,135-16- 9	- -
1792		D°		30,000	- -	46,339-18- 4	- -
1793		D°			- -	57,732- 4-11	- -
1794		D°		9,800	- -	42,429- 7-10	- -
1795		D°		40,300	- -	65,716- 6- 7	- -
1796		5 Shillings	500	61,450	171-12- 0	34,473- 6- 8	108- 1-11
1797	30,000	No Dividend			1,271-12- 0	32,677- 4-10	954- 8-11
1798		D°			1,084- 1- 0	8,700-12-11	711-16- 1
1799	70,000	D°			915- 7- 2	68,737-13- 6	996-11- 3
1800		D°			1,064- 4- 3	7,136- 0- 4	1,583- 5- 3
1801		D°		142,900	1,186- 5- 5	14,365- 0- 9	1,958- 2- 0
1802		D°			1,473- 6- 0	75,629- 2-10	2,724- 1- 8
1803		D°		91,000	1,338-11- 4	43,611- 7-11	1,832- 1- 0
1804		D°		12,200	1,368- 6- 6	82,784-11- 7	2,948-12- 3
1805		D°		83,250	1,426- 5- 2	74,034- 2- 8	3,306-19- 8
1806		D°		155,200	1,730-17- 9	80,653- 0- 1	4,372-10- 5
1807		D°		76,000	3,730-14-11	73,098- 8-10	9,989-13- 2
1808		One Pound	3,000	49,600	4,363-12- 2	39,730-15-11	13,021-16- 5
1809		Two Pounds	6,000	79,900	4,223- 0- 2	16,978-14- 7	12,599- 0- 5
1810		Two Pounds	6,000	10,950	4,586- 8- 9	14,458- 3- 6	15,024-10- 6
£	300,000	- -	15,500	842,550	29,934- 4- 7	930,805- 3-11	72,131-11- 4

Index

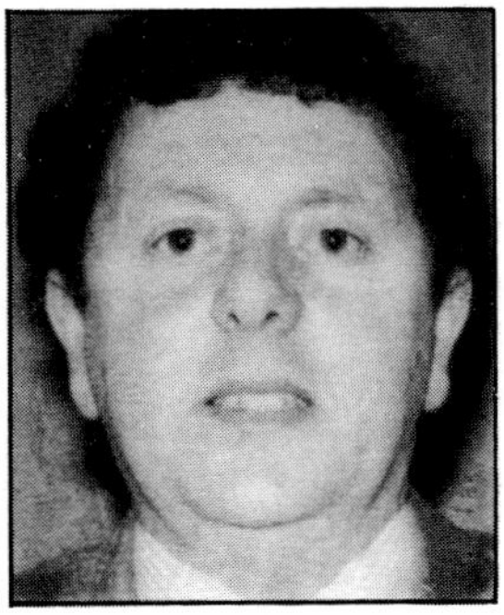

Peter Clarke

Peter Clarke was born in Dublin in 1949 and is married to Catherine Greville. They have three children, Peter, Damien and Eleanor. He is a school teacher by profession and is a graduate of Trinity College, Dublin.

An active member of the Royal Canal Amenity Group, he conducts guided tours and walks on the Royal Canal on behalf of the group.

Over the last number of years he has lectured and given talks on the history of the Royal Canal.

He was awarded a Masters Degree in Science for his thesis 'The Royal Canal 1789-1991'.

Cover Photographs:
Front cover: 22nd lock at Riverstown Bridge, county Westmeath.
Back cover: Section of the Killucan flight viewed through 20th lock.